TRADITIONAL ARAN KNITTING

Shelagh Hollingworth

with a foreword by
Heinz Edgar Kiewe

DOVER PUBLICATIONS, INC.
Mineola, New York

Acknowledgement

The author would like to acknowledge the following who generously gave help, equipment and time in the preparation of this book: 3 Suisses, Emu Wools, Lister/Lee Ltd, Patons and Baldwins Ltd, Sirdar Ltd, H. G. Twilley Ltd and Wendy Wools. Mr Heinz Edgar Kiewe for permission to use his researches into the history of knitting and all the knitters who patiently made samples and garments, especially Joan Edwardes, Gillian Nuttall and Sheila Thomas.

Bibliographical Note

This Dover edition, first published in 2006, is a republication of the work originally published under the title *The Complete Book of Traditional Aran Knitting* by B. T. Batsford Ltd., London, in 1982. The list of suppliers has been omitted in this edition.

Library of Congress Cataloging-in-Publication Data

Hollingworth, Shelagh.
    [Complete book of traditional Aran knitting]
    Traditional Aran knitting / Shelagh Hollingworth with a foreword by Heinz Edgar Kiewe.
        p. cm.
    Originally published: The complete book of traditional Aran knitting. London : B.T. Batsford, 1982, 1983 printing.
    Includes index.
    ISBN 0-486-44807-X (pbk.)
    1. Knitting—Ireland—Aran Islands—Patterns. I. Title.

TT819.I74A724 2005
746.43'2'0941748—dc22

2005053702

Manufactured in the United States of America
Dover Publications, Inc., 31 East 2nd Street, Mineola, N.Y. 11501

Contents

Foreword

By Heinz Edgar Kiewe

It gives me great pleasure to have been invited to introduce the first complete book of traditional Aran knitting. Nearly 50 years ago Robert Flaherty's splendid film, 'Man of Aran', opened the door for me to a new philosophy of man. For the distinguished American director, the island folk were his entire cast. Their life belonged to what my school training dismissed as an illiterate world. But suddenly I realised that for thousands of years illiterate people had lived perhaps a more tranquil, a fairer way of life.

Growing up, I had observed the lives of stags, of chickens, of dogs and cats. All had the qualities of a family instinct, showing care and love and loyalty without benefit of literacy. These Aran seamen and their families seemed to have their inborn qualities, too, passing on their wisdom and experience without need of the written word. They had met strangers on the ocean and exchanged their catches of fish for spices, as I discovered, as far away as Maroc. Skilfully they stretched sheepskins over their boats and spun their wool to make their unique and practical clothing which was their passport and their identity document, expressing their background through its coils and curves more vividly than cold words could manage.

There, in sign language, was the evidence of their origins and the things that gave meaning to their lives, symbols of family and faith. A typical Aran design consists of a centre panel with two side panels bordered with cable, signifying the ropes or lifelines on which a fisherman's life might depend.

Even now, many of the meanings are lost. But the islanders belonged to a civilised heritage guarded by the cosmopolitan Celts while European art and culture was being obliterated in the early centuries after Christ. Their values were protected in the symbolism of their textiles. They came from the forgotten generations of Celtic tribes who wandered across continents for thousands of years, perhaps from Eastern Turkey along the Danube to settle in what is now Bohemia and spreading westwards to France or Belgium and across comparatively safe water to the seclusion of Ireland and Aran. Since the monastery was set up on Aran in 530, they may have sailed as far as Egypt and back.

And that seamanship must be a clue to the coded messages of the chunky sweaters made from untreated creamy wool. As sailors they were ropemakers. They twisted and corded strands of hemp. They strung the ropes, folding them once, twice or three times. They folded them lengthways and braided them. They girded them round holy men, carved them into Celtic loops and hailed them in the shape of the Holy Cross.

That could bridge the gaps of understanding that words can open up between people speaking different languages. With symbols for every law and proverb of their tradition, they could make themselves understood to Celts all over central Europe. Until the beginning of this century it was the men who knitted, while the women spun the wool. A garment could incorporate the symbol of their family, the signs of blessing and of defence. Like Jacob, they wrestled symbolically with the angel of the Lord, expressed in a vertical twist of cables. Their holy signs were recognised everywhere. When they appear on the white knitted stockings of Austria or Switzerland—where Irish monasteries were well established by around 500—it was no coincidence. The Irish Celts had founded the Schotten Kloster in Vienna and the monastery of St Gallen.

Seamen of England knitted similar styles, less flamboyant and graceful. They are called Ganseys, after Guernsey. The colour was navy blue. In France I was told that the dyes 100 years ago were French navy, and better. They reached England's coast by way of Guernsey. But the Aran kept their knitting in natural white wool. They knew it kept them warmer, even when their currach collapsed and plunged them into icy water for a night.

I know now that the patterns are thousands of years old, though it took Trinity College in Dublin a decade to confirm my discovery that Daniel in the Book of Kells wore Aran-patterned knitted stockings, breeches and sweater, though by then they had forgotten the name of the discoverer of that Irish tale. If Aran was an important centre for the style that bears its name, it will not have been the only one. Like Oxford English, Aran knitting is a standard. History does not tell the stories properly. Much remains to be discovered about those wise and proud illiterates. It will have to be pieced together as an archeologist rebuilds a shattered pot. This is a task for today's young people, who are delightedly making their own discoveries about the neglected pioneers of the past, whose achievements still speak without words.

1982

Introduction

All stitch patterns, no matter how complicated the finished appearance, have their beginnings in simple knit or purl.

From the time we learn these two basic stitches we strive to produce examples of our work worthy of our skill. Frequently a knitter will make the Aran garment the highest challenge of his or her knitting craft and, having made this exhibition piece, will leave the knitting scene.

Who first invented those fascinating convolutions of the knitting now synonymous with the Aran Islands? We shall probably never know. We can only be grateful and follow their ingenuity by preserving those patterns and, perhaps, adding a few of our own.

A great fund of pattern stitches exists today, many more than can be covered by this one book, and new ones are developed every day. This book is for those who are novices to Aran knitting, for the experienced knitter and for the adventurous who would like to create a completely individual garment to their own design.

Do not despair if you should make a mistake in knitting your first piece of Aran knitting—this is probably how many of the stitches were originally discovered; today's mistake may be tomorrow's delight.

Child's sweater with crossover shawl collar, pattern 14

1 About the Aran Islands

The origin of the famous patterns of the Aran Islands is lost in antiquity but the reasons for the arrival of the fishing 'shirt', or sweater as it is commonly called today, may be easily understood when the geography and history of the Islands is considered.

The Islands lie to the west coast of Ireland in the mouth of Galway Bay, and to their west they are exposed to the Atlantic Ocean. This geographical position has much to bear on the condition of the landscape and the way in which generations of the islanders have made their subsistence living in the past.

There are three main islands in the group, Inishmore, the largest, lying to the North, Inishmaan (or middle Island) and Inisheer, the island to the south-eastern point of the three.

Although life could never have been said to be good on the islands, there have always been fluctuations in its population. Until about the early eighteenth century the Aran islands played a very important role in the defence of the Western coast of Ireland but later, when strategy altered, the people had to fall back on their subsistence farming and fishing with which we usually associate them. The land consisted mainly of rocky outcrops with small patches of workable soil. The islanders laboured hard and, by making dry stone walls surrounding tiny fields and, in some cases, bringing turf and seaweed to form these fields, managed to raise a few crops and rear hardy cattle on the land. With this and the fishing, which had since time immemorial provided food for the islanders and for the mainland, they were able to maintain a meagre living. Indeed, during the terrible potato famine in Ireland and at times when the mainland was heavily forested and boggy, conditions were so much better on the islands that it was easier to travel across by sea and settle on the islands.

As the mainland began to become more built up and industry developed, bringing better opportunities and living conditions, the emigration from the islands began again. Early in the twentieth century the younger folk left the islands hoping to make their fortune, not just on the mainland but as far away as the United States of America. During the decades leading up to the 1970s the population had dwindled to a quite alarming number. However, with the recent trend towards self-sufficiency, many of the islanders have begun to return to their birthplace and, hopefully, the population will begin a new ascent.

For these people their adventure is cushioned by the helpful wonders of the latest technology and they have the best of both worlds. For them there is the peace and the knowledge that they are making a proud and independent living as hundreds of islanders have in the past, together with the comfort of modern day communication and all the benefits that it provides, the speed of air travel, instant contact by telephone with the mainland and, should distraction be desired, the instant entertainment of radio, television and audio systems.

The cattle that were raised on the islands in the past were part of the income of the people; they were shipped to the mainland for a sufficiently good price to make it worth their while. Until fairly recently this shipment was quite a spectacle and of great fascination to the visitor as well as entertainment to the local people. Because there was no pier in those days on Inishmaan and Inisheer, the cattle were obliged to swim out to the mailboat (the regular caller) and to be winched aboard. Gradually this scene will disappear; a pier has been begun at Inisheer and in just a few years this will be, except for photographs, an historical oddity.

Visitors to the islands are made very welcome and tourism is quite a thriving industry. Although geographically they are relatively small, the islands offer much to see. They are steeped in history and any tourist on the west coast of Ireland should consider a visit to the islands an almost vital part of their tour while they are in the area. Arriving by air the whole pattern is laid out: the great cliffs of Inishmore, the limestone plateau and the historical sites, the famous stone forts and the remains of the monasteries and half buried churches. Visitors come from all over the world, many of them students of ancient languages, as this is part of the Irish-speaking district—the Gaeltacht—where the purest old Irish is still spoken. There are still the old fishing curraghs, canvas successors of the frail pre-historic skin-covered craft; still the rough cowhide pampooties—hand made leather, sandal-type shoes that have to be dampened occasionally to keep them supple—the brightly coloured crios—a long hand woven belt worn round the waist by the men—and, of course, the Aran knitting.

Famous though the knitting is, the idea of a great cottage industry is far from a true one. Unfortunately the remuneration from hand knitting is very small related to the time taken to produce a garment; add to this the expense of importing the yarn and all that remains is a few garments to attract the tourists. The bulk of the work that is sent all over the world has to be done by workers on the mainland.

When the patterns were first 'discovered' and admired as

works of art as well as for their functional quality they earned their authenticity and rarity because the patterns had never been committed to anything but memory. Now that a generally accepted knitting notation has been formed and many of the pattern stitches and garment shapes have been recorded, it is no longer necessary to go to the Aran islands for the sweaters. They can be purchased anywhere in the world and may be hand knitted by those with the ability, but because of the skill and resourcefulness of the islanders of the past this type of work will always be known by the distinctive name of Aran knitting.

2 Development of Aran knitting

When we have learnt a little of the history, geography and way of life in the past for the Aran islanders it is easy to understand how the garments and the stitches may have come about.

The fishing shirts were originally made as a protection against the elements. The men were out in all weathers, fishing from their curraghs and later from heavier fishing vessels, in terrible seas such as were shown in the famous film of the Aran fishermen, 'Man of Aran'. It was known that wool had certain waterproof properties. Technology can now prove that what these people knew by experience is borne out by fact.

Possibly the most important feature in the make up of wool is its ability to absorb moisture without feeling wet. What is more, when it does absorb moisture, it gives out heat. Therefore, a fisherman's sweater, when it gets wet (provided the knitting texture is close) will not only keep the wearer dry but also warm. The somewhat complex fibre contained in wool consists of a series of scales, known as epithelial scales. These, when seen under a microscope, show that the scales overlap one another, lapping more, or less, according to the particular breed of sheep. In the same way that water flows over a tile roof without entering, so moisture is inclined to flow over the scales without penetrating.

One result of this type of structure is that, when the fibre is stretched, the scales draw together and on release they return to the original formation, thus making an elastic and resilient fibre. Furthermore, wool makes a splendid insulating material. By their nature, the individual fibres are able to trap air within the fleece while it is on the sheep's back, keeping the sheep warm in winter and cool in summer. This ability is not lost in spinning since the basic fibre construction does not alter, and this natural insulation is yet another advantage of wool.

Finally, the other protective quality of wool, which is not retained in wool for general use, is the natural grease it contains. This is a secretion of the sebaceous glands in the sheep's skin close to the wool follicles. This grease is useful to the hand spinner since it helps the fibres to cling together, but it is also useful when left in the yarn used for fishermen's sweaters to be used in rough weathers because it adds to the waterproofing effect of the fabric. (However, the oil content is reduced with successive washes.) This wool can be purchased ready for knitting and is called oiled wool, as opposed to scoured wool which has had the oil (or the greater part of it) removed.

Those who were able to make a living by fishing worked at that industry and some of those who remained at home tended the sheep. These hardy sheep produced just the right type of wool for spinning into the waterproof, slightly rough, yarn that is only slightly more refined these days, and it protected the men and animals alike against the same elements. By the time it had had some of the dirt and grease removed (part scouring) it had become the creamy natural colour (bainin) with which we are all familiar, and although the patterns are worked in other fashion colours and yarns, the true Aran is only made from the thickish bainin woollen yarn.

It has been mentioned that to keep the garment virtually waterproof, in addition to its natural properties, it is necessary to work the stitches closely. It is probably from this necessity that the beginnings of the fancy patterns were made. It will be obvious that the tighter one knits that basic of all patterns, stocking stitch, the finer will become any space between the stitches but, at the same time, in practice, this will produce a fabric as hard and as uncomfortable as a board. However, when one takes the weaving process of knitting a stage further and crosses the stitches this doubly enhances the scaled surfaces. It lessens the chance of inflow of moisture and with the weave entraps the air in the same way as the basic fibre, adding to the insulating properties. By cabling and twisting the stitches we not only eliminate the need for a board-like garment but we finish with a wearable sweater with all the characteristics of the wool itself— waterproofing, insulation and elasticity. We have created a functional piece of knitting and that alone is worth doing but, more happily, we have also created a thing of beauty. Without doubt, the shapes and patterns of the Aran knitting when put together in one sweater or similar piece of knitting make a remarkable collection of textures, sometimes almost a bas-relief sculpture.

The origin of the very first patterns cannot now be found but research into the general history of knitting and, in particular, Aran knitting has brought forth some very interesting speculation. The most generally accepted theory of the symbols in various patterns is that they are based on religious themes. When the geographical position of the islands is considered and one remembers their importance in the centuries of defence to the western coast of Ireland, it is obvious that it would be a natural calling place for all types of travellers, monks, merchants, explorers, etc. These people would bring with them items of other cultures, bearing religious symbols, even before Christianity, geometric shapes, lozenges, braids and zigzag lines, and in the same manner the knitting style that these travellers had evolved would have found its way to other countries. It has been seen that the bobble patterns and diamonds are still worked in parts of Germany, and they possibly had a common origin with Aran knitting. The simple cable patterns have been worked all over the world by many nations and indeed, before the sudden popularity of Aran knitting in the 1940s, the cable pattern was frequently seen on the ubiquitous cricket sweater. This journeying of the patterns, relayed purely by demonstration since there is no written record, is the most likely link between the knitting patterns and symbols of the world. As for the meanings, these are various and many become even more obscure as the names of the stitches are handed down.

The eminent knitting historian Heinz Edgar Kiewe has done much to try and disentangle the mystery of the symbols and suggests these religious meanings:

Interlacing or trellis—the bond of man with God and religion (person bound by monastic vows, etc.)

Plaits—the holy three strands of hair ribbon or straw, the plaited holy bread of the Old Testament, symbolic of a devout family bound up with God.

Tree of life or ladder of life—Jacob's dream of the ladder to heaven.

Holy Trinity pattern—this pattern, made by making one of three and three of one, is attributed to the message on St Patrick's breastplate—'I bind unto myself today the strong name of the Trinity by invocation of the same, three in one and one in three.'

These are religious meanings of some of the symbols and a religious connection can be traced via the merchant routes and the travelling of the monks from and to the very eastern end of the Mediterranean. In his printed notes on his research into Aran knitting Heinz Edgar Kiewe also gives some of the more romantic explanations for the decorative ornaments the craftsmen in ancient Irish knitting use:

Zigzag—knit stitches moving diagonally across a purl panel and used to represent the twisting cliff paths along the shore.

Double zigzag—also known as marriage lines, usually considered symbolic of the ups and downs of married life.

Cables—these are of all types and represent the fisherman's ropes.

Tree of life—this pattern is worked by knit or twist stiches forming a trunk and branches against a purl background, and signifies long life and strong sons to carry on the fisherman's work.

The ladder of life—purl or twist stitches are worked to form the poles and rungs of the ladder against a knit stitch background. It is usually considered symbolic of man's earthly climb to eternal happiness.

The Trellis—an intricate pattern of knit stitches worked to form a trellis effect over purl stitches and representing the small fields enclosed with stone walls found in the west of Ireland. Along the west coast of Ireland many of the fishermen had their own individual pattern, the romantic Victorian tale being that if the men were drowned in the constant gales that lash the Western coast, they could be identified by the patterns on their sweaters.

Holy Trinity stitch—sometimes known as blackberry stitch. This is made by making 'three from one and one from three' across the panel.

Honeycomb—this looks exactly like its name and is made by twisting stitches forward and back across the panel. It was considered symbolic of hard work bringing its just reward, as the work of the busy bee produces the golden honey.

Spoon stitch—lover's spoon—lover's pattern?

As well as these romantic explanations and the Christian religious possibilities it must be added that some of the designs are to be found on ancient Celtic crosses and symbols that pre-date Christianity. Without doubt, in the dark ages the islands suffered from visits from the Vikings, who would have brought yet more varieties of symbols with them. Wherever there is an element of design in history, unless the meaning has been passed down with folklore, the pattern remains and the reasons for its being pass into obscurity.

We are fortunate that only the meanings of the symbols have faded and not the patterns themselves. These were preserved originally simply by being passed down in families from mother to daughter; it was the women who did the knitting on the islands, not the men. Various reasons have been given for the patterns not having been recorded; some say that the families were jealous of their own pattern and did not wish to let it go or that, having secured this method of keeping the men of the family identifiable by the pattern, would not risk using a different one.

While both of these reasons could be true, it is also probable that when learning to knit the patterns, which must have been quite a daunting task when there were no written instructions to refer to, a young girl had enough to do to remember just the patterns that were familiar to her mother without trying to grasp a new design of her neighbour's. As the Aran knitter will be aware, it takes quite some time to become accustomed to working the particular patterns of a garment and they must be un-learned before the next sweater can be worked.

One theory of how the sweaters developed so many panels is that a woman working a stocking stitch sweater with only a centre panel was a newcomer to that family, usually a bride from another part of the island. This she would be knitting for her first born so that he might wear it when he joined his father in the fishing boat. Then, when the next son came along, another panel would be added at each side. By the time the grandchildren arrived, new panels would be added to the central patterns and in this way the tradition was perpetuated in the family. In those days not only were the women too busy to allow for learning new patterns but their education would not have allowed for any method of notating the patterns. It was not until instructions began to take on their present day style that sufficient interest began to be taken in the stitch patterns and proper preservation could be made.

Although an example of Aran knitting is illustrated in the ancient Irish *Book of Kells* in A.D. 820 the earliest piece of Aran knitting properly recorded and photographed was as recent as 1936. This was a 'peculiar whiskery looking chunk of a sweater in biblical white at St Stephen's Green in Dublin', purchased by Heinz Edgar Kiewe. This was identified as a sample of cable stitches and a photograph of it was published in Mary Thomas's *Book of Knitting Patterns*. As has been stated, before this time the only popular Aran patterns used widely were cables which had been used, together with moss stitch, on Jerseys and Guernseys and other fishing sweaters. Mr Kiewe feels that this may have been the beginnings of the upsurge of interest in the Aran patterns which have evolved into such an infinite variety today. Many of the modern day designs owe little to the authentic patterns, but each has a little place in the enormous, never-ending concept of knitting ingenuity.

3 Equipment and working methods

The instructions in this book are not designed for the genuine beginner to knitting. It is accepted that a small amount of experience should be gained before embarking upon a garment of relatively advanced difficulty. The knitter who knows something of the craft will already have mastered the basics: casting on and off, knit stitch and purl stitch, increasing and decreasing.

EQUIPMENT
Yarns
Authentic knitting patterns for Aran stitches in fisherman style sweaters should be worked in wool. The weight of the wool, or its quality, is somewhat thicker than double knitting weight. There are four strands to its make-up but it should never be confused with four-ply wool. The term 'Aran knitting wool' generally refers to this thicker yarn, sometimes with a slightly rough or hairy texture, and most frequently it is stocked in the natural or bainin (pronounced bawneen) colour. Some spinners specialise in producing a yarn as close to the original as possible, while others spin the yarn to a more refined standard yet to the same thickness and possibly to a slightly creamier colour.

A perfectly acceptable machine-washable yarn has been used for some of the garments in this book to demonstrate that the beauty of the stitches is not lost when they are worked in other types of yarn. This machine-washable quality is highly suitable for those allergic to wool.

The attractive appearance of the stitches should not be retained solely for sportswear and rugged garments. The gold waistcoat worked in a luxury yarn (pattern 16) shows how effective the patterns look when translated into fashion wear. Try experimenting with other luxury yarns, such as mohair and cashmere; the raised effect of the patterns is enhanced by the lustre of these yarns. The simplest of the cable patterns can look very pretty on babies' wear and toddlers' clothes, but smaller patterns should be used relative to the three-ply, four-ply or double knitting yarn being used.

Washing yarns
It is most important to read the washing instructions on the ball band of the yarn before attempting to wash your Aran

garments. It is generally safe to hand wash most yarns but care must be taken. Try not to let hand knitted garments get really dirty because the washing process should only be a gentle motion through delicate suds in hand-hot water. Vigorous rubbing to loosen dirt will result in a hard, matted surface and will mar the look of the patterns that you have worked so hard to produce. A fisherman's sweater is usually heavy in weight, even when dry; after washing it will have absorbed a great deal of water and will be very heavy indeed. It may not be harmed by a very short spin in a spin drier to take out the initial amount of excess water, but in no circumstances should a woollen garment be put into a tumble drier as the hot tumbling action is liable to mat or felt the fabric.

If possible, dry the garment flat. There are various drying nets available these days that can be laid over the bath so that the garment will drip through the net without dragging any particular part out of shape, as can sometimes happen when sweaters are hung up to dry. If hanging the sweater up cannot be avoided, it is preferable to hang it suspended by the join at the armpit rather than the welt or shoulders. In this way any peg mark will not show and the weight of the sweater is better distributed. It is not advisable to fold a sweater across the body over a clothes line; this invariably leaves a crease which is virtually impossible to press out without spoiling the character of the Aran patterns.

When you purchase the yarn try to buy the whole quantity at once. Even with a yarn in a cream or natural shade there can be variations in the batches or dye lots, and mixing with another wool lot at a later stage will almost certainly show in the finished garment, no matter how close the colours look in the ball.

Knitting needles

When knitting authentic fishing sweaters and sportswear in Aran quality yarns the thicker end of the range of knitting needles will be called for. The sizes of needles depends on the thickness of the yarn and the relative tension (gauge) obtained by the knitter; this is dealt with in the section on tension.

The thickness of the yarn will make for quite a large number of thick loops (stitches) on the needles and for this type of work a long length of knitting needle is advisable. For working Aran patterns in finer grades of yarn smaller needles may be used if preferred.

When a genuine fishing shirt is completed to the collar stage it will be necessary to work the collar in rounds of knitting and some sets of four double-pointed needles will be required. Most of the modern knitted variations are joined at one shoulder only before working the neckband or collar and for these the normal pair of two single-ended needles are suitable.

The other vital piece of needle equipment for the knitter of Aran patterns is, of course, the cable needle. This is a short needle, pointed at both ends. They are usually sold in sets, sometimes of two needles, each of a different thickness, the thicker suitable for working with the thick Aran quality yarns and double knittings and the finer for use with fine yarns and needles. This is the needle with which the knitter will be able to twist the stitches to the front or back of the work to form the famous twists and cable patterns.

Needle gauge

The change to metric measurements for knitting needles has taken place over the past few years. A chart showing the comparative sizes is given at the back of this book, but if you are not certain of the size of a needle there are needle gauges available at most wool stores or haberdashery counters and this will help you to measure the needles; they are generally metal or plastic with holes or slots with the correct needle size marked by each size.

Stitch holders

These small accessories are useful in the knitter's work basket. Where a pattern instructs that stitches must be left for the time being, e.g. at the back neck of a sweater, it is usually more convenient to leave them on a stitch holder than on the spare needles since the holder is smaller and will trap the stitches in place until required. When working the collar it is a simple movement to slip the stitches back on to a needle.

Row counters

With Aran knitting, more than any other type of knitting, the row counter is essential. This is a small cylindrical counter that slips on to the end of one knitting needle. The most effective method of using it is to place it at the end of the needle working the right side rows; then, at the end of the wrong side row as the work is passed from the right to the left hand, the row counter passes through the fingers reminding the knitter to notch up two more rows.

Most of the Aran knitting designs have more than one fancy panel to be worked at the same time as another. These do not necessarily have the same number of rows, therefore the row counter is a useful check. It is of course very useful when the work has to be put down and left for a while.

Tape measure

All types of knitting require measuring and a good tape measure is vital. The basic tension must be measured before the article is begun and the overall measurements must be checked while the work is being made. When designing your own sweaters etc. the need for a good, unstretching tape measure (e.g. fibreglass) cannot be over-stressed.

A metric/imperial tape measure can be purchased at most good wool stores and haberdashers' counters and may help knitters to cope with measurement problems until he or she is accustomed to metric measurements. When working the patterns in this book use only metric or imperial measurements; do not try to combine the two.

Crochet hooks

For garments without ribbed welts or borders a neat row of double crochet will serve to trim an otherwise uneven line. A medium-sized crochet hook is a useful item to keep handy in the work box for this purpose and for those anxious moments when a dropped stitch needs picking up.

Pressing equipment

The best surface for pressing highly-patterned articles such as those composed of Aran patterns is a table covered first by a folded blanket, or similar fabric, with a suitable clean cotton cloth secured on top. The average ironing board is rather too narrow to support all of a garment at one time.

A steam iron may be used for pressing, but the more old-fashioned method of warm iron over a damp cloth is still preferable for the true Aran wools.

Always read the pressing instructions on the ball band. Some of the modern mixtures of yarns, especially those that have some synthetic content, require pressing with a cool iron, sometimes over a dry cloth, and in some instances they should not be pressed at all.

If pressing is suggested in the making up instructions only press the pieces lightly; too much pressure will flatten the patterns and spoil the very effect of relief patterning that the knitter has been striving for. The ribbed sections must also be omitted in the pressing since too heavy a pressing will elimate much of the elasticity of the ribbing and may even cause sagging or fluting of the welts, cuffs or collars.

Note book and paper

The note book will be useful for noting down favourite patterns, measurements (your own and members of the family) and other details, such as how many rows you have worked on the back of a sweater so that you will work the front to the same row, or you may want to write in the dye lot number of the yarn you are using or the washing/pressing instructions so that you will not need to keep the ball band long after you have completed the garment.

Knitters have their own personal methods for arranging their knitting for Aran work. A popular way to organize the patterns so that they may be read across at one glance is to take a wide sheet of paper, mark it out in columns, one for each Aran panel, and write the pattern in the column below. In this way the necessity of turning back and forth between the pages is avoided.

Sewing needles

Finally, garments in the thick yarns, such as Aran weight and chunky yarns, should be sewn with a matching finer yarn, such as four-ply, used with a knitter's blunt-tipped sewing needle.

WORKING METHODS

Tension

Knitters who have reached a sufficiently advanced stage of expertise to undertake working Aran knitting patterns will already be aware that tension is the measurement of the number of stitches and rows to a given number of centimetres or inches when a particular type of yarn is worked on a certain size of needle. The designer experiments with a portion of that yarn on various sizes of needle until she finds a texture that feels correct—not too tight and not too loose. She then notes how many stitches and rows there are on this sample to, say, 10 cm (4 in), and the needle size required to obtain the square. It is upon this measurement that the whole of the design will be based, therefore it is essential that the knitter also experiments, using the same quality of yarn and various sizes of knitting needles, until she too can produce the same tension measurements, otherwise the finished article is unlikely to be to the same standard or specification.

Many of the patterns in this book, especially those in Aran-type yarns, are worked to a similar tension, but because the yarn itself is different the needles used to obtain the tension may be different. The tension square for Aran patterns is frequently given in stocking stitch. This is because the twisting and weaving of the various patterns draws in some panels more than others and it is not possible to give a standard tension that will cover all of the panels in one sweater. Where the stocking stitch tension is given, the alteration caused by the twisting of the stitches has been allowed for in the design. Find which needles will produce the stocking stitch tension and use these needles for the patterned work and the result should be a correctly fitting garment.

It should be realized that the twisting and cabling of stitches will produce a fabric that is somewhat more rigid than normal patterned knitting, therefore it is customary to work these patterns with more stitches than for a similar size of flat patterned work. The patterns in this book have been adjusted accordingly.

Cable Knitting

This form of twisting the stitches, originally devised to resemble the ropes used by fisherfolk, is the very basis upon which most of the patterns are formed. The traditional simple cable pattern looks very much like a rope in the way that it twists around itself and stands out against the surface of the plain background of the knitting.

To fashion these cable patterns, no matter how devious they may appear, the method is always the same. The cable consists of a certain number of stitches which are divided so that some of that number may be twisted around the others by the use of a cable needle. To twist the stitches out of their normal knitting order a given number of stitches must be taken either to the front or the back of the work on to the cable needle and left there while the stitches from the main needle are worked; then the stitches from the cable needle may be either slipped back on to the main needle to be worked or worked directly from the cable needle.

The number of stitches in the cable is usually divided equally and the cable notation will cover the total number of stitches in use, not just the number to be set on to the cable needle. In other words, C. 8.F., cable eight stitches front thus: slip next 4 sts. to front on cable needle, k.4, k.4 from cable needle. In some of the more Archaic Aran patterns an uneven number of stitches is cabled and at uneven intervals, but the method is the same as given for the even numbers and regular intervals.

1 *Slip 4 sts. to back on cable needle*

2 *K. 4 sts. on main needle*

3 *K. 4 sts. from cable needle*

4 *Slip 4 sts. to front on cable needle, then k.4 from main needle*

5 *K. 4 sts. from cable needle*

6 *Cable 8 back, cable 8 front*

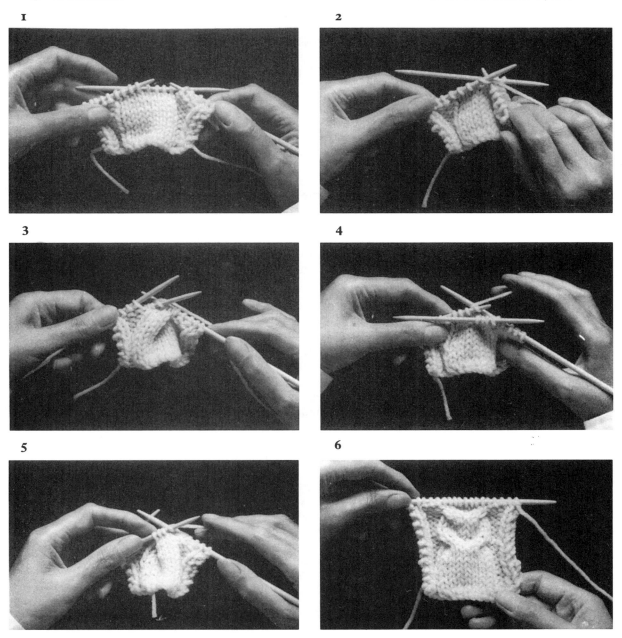

1   2

3   4

5   6

Occasionally a pattern will give instructions for twisting stitches or crossing stitches. There are various methods for twisting the positions of two adjacent stitches, some of these taking the twist over two rows, others only on the right side of the work. Instructions for twist stitches and cross stitches are given individually in each pattern as they occur because the method of twist is dependent on the direction in which the cord effect is to turn.

Special cable instructions are given at the beginnings of many of the patterns and samples in this book because the variations in the more complicated patterns are so numerous that the knitter would waste considerable time constantly referring to the abbreviations section.

It should not be assumed that abbreviations, such as F.Cr. (Front Cross) indicate the same method on every pattern. The special abbreviations before any pattern should be individually studied since the abbreviation may have been used to cover a different method of twisting the stitches from a previous pattern or sample.

Bobbles

A favourite way of decorating the Aran garment is by working raised knots, clusters or, as they are most commonly known, bobbles. These bobbles stand out well against a plain background but are also very effective when used in conjunction with the other popular shapes: diamonds and cables, etc. They are fairly slow to work but are frequently so much part of the integral design that the patient Aran knitter will be pleased to make the finished article even more elaborate by this extra work.

There are many ways of forming the bobbles; the special instructions at the beginning of each pattern or sample must be noted since there are at least six different methods used in this book.

Choosing and following a pattern

When choosing the first pattern for your initial venture into Aran patterns avoid those that have a great number of panels. There are plenty of commercial patterns simply with central Aran patterns surrounded by stocking stitch and these are usually the best for a beginner.

The more experienced knitter may be prepared to tackle a very complicated design but even she would be well advised to work a small portion of each panel first, separately, so that any misunderstandings over the technicalities may be worked out over a small section of work rather than in the middle of a garment.

Read through the intructions first, making sure that you understand all the special abbreviations as well as those generally listed at the beginning of the book.

Before beginning any pattern, *check your tension* by the method outlined on page 22. Even if you have made this particular garment before the tension must be checked again;

it is possible that your tension may have altered or there may be a very slight difference in the yarn.

Organizing the work

As has already been suggested in the section on equipment on page 21, it is a good idea to arrange a sheet of paper into columns and to write in the pattern rows below each pattern heading. Apart from the ease with which the patterns can then be read, it is a simple task to place a tick in the column below after a certain number of rows has been completed. This plan can also be used to write in full the side pattern stitches in the appropriate columns after, for example, the armhole shaping, since the pattern rows at this stage seldom begin and end in the original way as given after the rib welt.

It is usually wise to work a pattern in the order in which it has been printed. The first section may contain specific instructions which are repeated in other sections or adapted elsewhere. It is usual for the first printed section to have all the instructions fully written and the other pieces linked to that, in which case it may be necessary to work out the first secton before embarking upon the remaining parts.

The notebook will prove very useful for the Aran knitter; it will help her to remember various small details of rows and stitches, for this knitting is too complex for her to rely on memory alone.

Aran knitting undoubtedly requires a high degree of concentraion; sometimes even a momentary distraction will cause an error, but the rewards that dedication to this type of intricate work can bring are long-lasting and satisfying.

Abbreviations

The following are the abbreviations normally used in knitting patterns. Any special abbreviations are given in the text of the pattern.

cm	centimetre(s)	rep.	repeat
dec.	decrease(ed) (ing)	st.(s.)	stitch(es)
in	inch(es)	st.-st.	stocking stitch
inc.	increase (ed) (ing)	t.b.l.	through back of loop
k.	knit	tog.	together
p.	purl	y.fwd.	yarn forward
p.s.s.o.	pass slip stitch over	y.bk.	yarn back

Size note

Figures before the square brackets are for the smallest of the listed sizes. Figures following between square brackets are for larger sizes. Where only one set of figures occurs this refers to all sizes. Imperial measurements follow the metric measurements in parentheses and are approximate. If you have trouble coping with metric measurements, buy a modern tape measure with both types of figures and convert the figures for your size before working, making a note of all the measurements in your note book.

4 Designing an Aran sweater

This section is not for the beginner, but the more experienced knitter may well reach a stage in her craft where she feels the need to try her skill at something even more advanced than the most difficult patterns at her command.

Designing your own fisherman's sweater is possibly the most rewarding task in hand knitting. Even the most elementary design worked to your personal choice of panels is a unique creation and, because of the method of constructing the sweaters in a series of panels, for which individual instructions are given, the basic fisherman sweater is relatively simple to design, without, for one's first efforts, much technical knowledge being necessary.

Before beginning any design it is necessary to have a list of the measurements of the finished pieces. For the first and most simple method of obtaining an original design it is best to select a pattern from this book that has been worked before and found to be satisfactory. Take the basic measurements from this garment.

Since this garment is going to assist you in your design it will help you to use the same yarn if possible. Work a tension sample as usual to ascertain which needles you will be using for your pattern work.

After the technical details at the beginning of each pattern there follows a list of the pattern panels used in that set of instructions. Each panel title is followed by a number of stitches required to work the particular pattern. This is where you can bring in your own personal touch. By taking a new panel from the selection of samples or from another pattern, provided the same number of stitches is required, the new pattern can, in most cases, be substituted.

This is a seemingly endless set of permutations but it is inadvisable to cast on the full number of stitches and merely substitute the new selection of patterns. Some panels do not form a good partnership with others; some will require a stocking stitch background and some will look better against reverse stocking stitch. Another important factor is that, despite having the same number of stitches to form the pattern, one pattern may knit up narrower than another owing to the variation in the twisting of the stitches. It is, therefore, vital to knit a sample of all the new stitches to be used and lie them side by side. You will be able to visualize the finished effect more easily and, by measuring the width of each sample, be able to calculate the total width of the piece of knitting.

If the width of the knitting is smaller than you require it is a simple task at this stage of the design to add a few link stitches between the panels. It is quite common for cable and other panels to have reverse stocking stitches between, partly to add to the raised effect of the patterns and frequently to contribute just a small amount to the overall measurement. Take care where these stitches are inserted; they are best between two columns of stocking stitch pattern. If they are set between panels that are already edged with reverse stocking stitch this will only form a wide, flat look detracting from the closely encrusted impact that Aran knitting generally has. Remember also to include these extra stitches at stocking stitch tension; they will not draw in as the Aran patterns will.

Having established this new set of patterns, cast on the stitches from the original pattern and continue as that pattern, using the shapings and allowing for any extra stitches. Do not leave the extra stitches to go in the neckline since this would probably make the neck too large and the underarm and shoulder rather narrow. It is better to distribute the added stitches evenly, with perhaps a third at the armhole shaping, a third in the shoulder shaping and the remaining stitches in the neckline.

This is a simple way of fashioning a garment that is totally personal, a completely original design, using the patterns that you have chosen. However, this is not the way the true designer works and you might like to create a design without having to refer to another pattern. The excitement and fun of choosing the panels that you want to use is even greater if you are not restricted to a particular number of stitches. Although many of the preliminary preparations for designing from scratch are rather technical, the advanced knitter will understand the need for them and the reasons may seem obvious.

It has been stated that before beginning a design measurements of all the pieces must be made. Fortunately the traditional fishing shirt is very plain in shape and the measurements can be kept to the minimum. Using your notebook note down the total chest measurement, length from shoulder to required lower edge, underarm length and width of upper arm.

Draw a diagram of the shape of the pieces; this need not be to scale but will help you calculate the stitches required. The width of the front and back will be half of the total chest measurement plus between 2·5 cm (1 in) and 5 cm (2 in) each on front and back to allow for movement; e.g. total chest measurement 102 cm (40 in); front of garment 51 cm (20 in) plus 3 cm (1¼ in); width calculated for front of garment 54 cm

Diagram 1 *Broken lines indicate essential measurements*

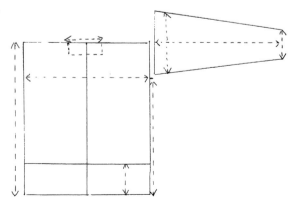

($21\frac{1}{4}$ in). The welt of a fisherman's sweater is longer than average, giving it a wide, short look; allow between 15 cm (6 in) up to 20 cm (8 in) according to the desired length. Above this comes the all important patterned section to the armhole. This measurement can be calculated by deducting from 23 cm (9 in)—for a small man—to 25 cm (10 in)—larger sizes—from the total length at the upper edge of the diagram and marking this point as the start of the armhole. There is no shaping for the underarm of the fishing sweater; the knitting is marked to indicate the armhole opening.

Mark a point 5 cm (2 in) below the shoulder since the shoulder line on these sweaters always forms lower than normal. This is because the sleeve top has an extension to fit across the shoulder edge, thus forming part of the front and back armhole depth. Draw a vertical line down the centre of the diagram and from this mark a point each side to indicate the neck width. This measurement should be taken from the back of the neck of the person for whom the garment is being designed.

The diagram for the sleeve shape will be a vertical rectangle, again, not necessarily to scale. The upper edge will be twice the depth allowed for the total armhole, e.g. total armhole depth 23 cm (9 in), top of sleeve 46 cm (18 in). The length of the sleeve will be as the underarm measurement. Width at cuff, between 23 cm (9 in) and 25 cm (10 in).

Work a tension sample in stocking stitch to your satisfaction. From these stitches work out how many would be required to be cast on for a front or back in stocking stitch. You will need this basic number to be cast on for the welts and cuffs etc. To do this, multiply the width measurement by the number of stitches to the cm (in). In the example given above, the number of stitches to be cast on for the front would be, at a tension of 20 sts. to 10 cm (4 in), 54 cm ($21\frac{1}{4}$ in) = 108 (107) sts.

It is usual and, because the Aran patterns draw inwards, desirable to increase the stitches on the row immediately following the welt. There is no set rule regarding the number of stitches that will be needed; this is dependent upon the panels that have been chosen. At this stage a large sheet of graph paper will be extremely useful. Mark a centre vertical line as the centre of the sweater front. From this central line mark out the number of stitches (each square representing a stitch) that you will need to form your chosen centre panel. If, for example, you have chosen a very ambitious panel of 36 stitches, you will count out 18 stitches at each side of the centre line. Next, count out on either side the next pattern and then another, not forgetting that some of these patterns will require the link stitches between them to make them stand out. Continue in this way until you have placed all of the panels you have chosen; there will usually be space for two or possibly three on each side of the centre panel. Measure the width of the panels, remembering that some o them will be used twice on the front. The difference between the width of the panels and the total chest requirement for the front will be worked plain at the side edges in any simple all over pattern, such as moss stitch, double moss stitch or reverse stocking stitch.

Below the columns now marked on the graph paper write the name of the pattern being used and call it panel A, B, C, etc. and add the total number of stitches. Add to this the extra stitches needed to obtain the full width, these to be calculated at stocking stitch tension. Let us suppose that after the centre panel of 36 stitches you have marked three separate panels of 9 stitches each, with 2 link stitches between and 2 stitches at the extreme outside edges; this will add 70 stitches to the centre 36 stitches. When you have measured the samples you may realize that they are 5 cm (2 in) short of the required width. Simply add 5 cm (2 in) multiplied by the number of stitches to the cm (in). At 20 sts. to 10 cm (4 in) this would add 10 stitches; the centre 36 stitches plus 70 pattern stitches = 116 stitches. Therefore after the welt is completed you will need to increase the stitches from 108 to 116 stitches. Since the front and back are worked alike you have achieved both sets of calculations at one go.

Diagram 2 *Basic shape of sections of traditional fishing shirt*

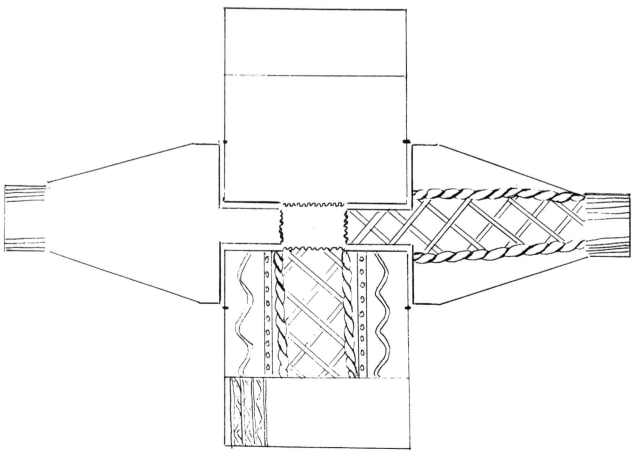

Continue to work on the patterns to the armhole measurement and mark both ends of this row to indicate the beginning of the armhole. It will greatly assist the knitting if the rows of the patterns are written in under the columns. Not all of the patterns begin and end on the same row and it is easier to keep a check on the pattern rows right across the work than to try to remember each time, especially if the work has to be set aside for a period.

After the armhole mark, for the back, continue until the lowered shoulder mark is reached (to allow for the sleeve extension). This drop in the shoulder line also affords extra depth to the neck opening. The neck stitches will be roughly the width you have marked on your diagram multiplied by the stocking stitch tension. e.g. 18 cm (7 in) multiplied by 20 sts. to 10 cm (4 in) will be 36 sts. You may appreciate that this will be a narrower width over your pattern stitches but this difference will compensate for the extra depth of the dropped shoulder line and the sleeve extension stitches which are included in the final collar stitches. It should also be noted that in this case the 36 stitches for the neck conveniently cover the central panel. This is customary and every endeavour should be made to fit a suitable number of stitches into the neck without detracting from the natural flow of the pattern.

Deduct the number of neck stitches from the total stitches and divide the remainder in two, one set for each shoulder. In our example we have 116 sts. less 36 sts. for the neck, leaving 80 sts.—40 sts. for each shoulder. Cast off the shoulder stitches straight at the beginning of the following two rows. Leave the remaining stitches on a stitch holder to be used later for the collar.

Plan the panels for the sleeves in the same way as for the back and front. It is not necessary to have the same patterns on the sleeves as on the back and front. Frequently a very elaborate pattern is used at the centre of the main parts and this will be too wide and over-decorative for the sleeves. Do not forget that the stitches required to make up the panels will be greater than the stitches calculated for the cuff and an increase row will have to be made.

Arrange a few stitches in a simple allover pattern at each edge if possible and, when increasing the stitches to widen the sleeve, this pattern can be continued up the sides. The difference in the width at the wrist and at the upper arm must be calculated at the stocking stitch tension since the increased stitches are worked in a flat pattern. The increases will take place quite rapidly to cover the full width between working the cuff and approximately 5 cm (2 in) from the top edge. You may find that you will need to increase 1 st. at both ends of every 4th row to accomplish all the increasing before the sleeve is the full length and 5 cm (2 in) is a desirable length of straight knitting before the cast off.

When the sleeve is the correct length, cast off the stitches straight at the beginning of the next two rows, leaving stitches to a width of approximately 10 cm (4 in) on the needle. Try to arrange the number of stitches to fall into an interesting part of the knitting so that the extension will form an integral part of the front and back shoulder shaping. Continue in the pattern as set on the extension stitches until this fits across the cast off shoulder edges of the back and front shoulders. Leave the stitches on a holder.

A set of four double pointed needles will be needed to work the collar of this type of sweater. First the sleeve extensions must be sewn to the cast off shoulder edges, then the stitches slipped from the holders on to the set of double-pointed needles and the collar worked in rounds of rib or a fancy rib pattern relating to the general theme of the work.

The cast off stitches at the sleeve top should fit neatly to the armhole above the marked row and sewn, then the side and sleeve seams can be joined.

It is fortunate that the traditional shape of the fishing sweater is such an uncomplicated one. Designing a sweater can be quite a daunting task, and combining that with some of the most intricate patterns in the world is possibly the greatest challenge that a knitter can undertake. However, with careful planning at the start your garment will soon begin to take shape and you will be on your way to producing a sweater that is totally your own design, made today and following a tradition, the beginnings of which are lost in time.

5 Aran pattern stitch samples

This is a selection of popular patterns that have been collected from numerous sources. Some are authentic and have been used to adorn fishing shirts for hundreds of years. Many others are relatively modern but make such a useful addition to the decorative whole that the nucleus of traditional designs can only be enhanced by their inclusion.

Very elaborate panels, such as those suitable as centres of heavily embossed sweaters, are often the result of an intricate weave of many simple stitch arrangements and, indeed, it is because of the very adaptability of the patterns that the permutations are endless. It is not possible to present a totally comprehensive list of all the Aran patterns available and the author apologises if a favourite has been left out. New patterns are being developed every day; the names of those that follow are sometimes traditional, almost classical, and occasionally the names given are those that have remained with the particular stitch combination, possibly because of their descriptive value.

The samples are not intended solely for reference or as a basis for fishermen's sweaters. They are all a decoration in their own right and will frequently blend happily with more unusual yarns to produce a novel range of textures. By experimenting with stitches and different yarns new and original fabrics may be fashioned. A favourite plain sweater pattern could be given a new lease of life with this form of interest but do remember to add between two and as many as eight extra stitches to compensate for any narrowing of the knitting.

It is wise to practise working the sample separately before incorporating it into any larger piece. These samples need not be wasted. A collection of samples worked to a common size will make up into a useful rug or an attractive cushion cover (see page 136).

If you should be fortunate enough to invent some entirely new patterns of your own it is a good idea to keep a separate notebook for them, mounting the sample swatch on one side of the page and writing the instructions on the adjacent page. In this way, unlike in the past when no doubt some of the patterns fell into disuse, we can keep a record of the stitches for all time.

7 *Four stitch cable back*

8 *Four stitch cable front*

9 *Six stitch cable back*

7   8   9

To clarify the instructions special abbreviations have been given with some of the samples.

SIMPLE CABLE PATTERNS

These first six samples are very old patterns; the theme for the design was probably taken from the construction of the ropes that the fishermen used. Similar symbols are also to be found on ancient Celtic crosses.

No. 1 Four Stitch Cable Front 8 sts.

1st row: (wrong side) K.2, p.4, k.2.
2nd row: P.2, k.4, p.2.
3rd row: As 1st row.
4th row: P.2, slip next 2 sts. to front on cable needle, k.2, then k.2 from cable needle, p.2.
These 4 rows form the pattern.

No. 2 Four Stitch Cable Back 8 sts.

1st row: (wrong side) K.2, p.4, k.2.
2nd row: P.2, k.4, p.2.
3rd row: As 1st row.
4th row: P.2, slip next 2 sts. to back on cable needle, k.2, then k.2 from cable needle, p.2.
These 4 rows form the pattern.

No. 3 Six Stitch Cable Front 10 sts.

1st row: (wrong side) K.2, p.6, k.2.
2nd row: P.2, k.6, p.2.
3rd row: As 1st row.
4th row: P.2, slip next 3 sts. to front on cable needle, k.3, then k.3 from cable needle, p.2.
5th to 8th rows: Repeat 1st and 2nd rows twice more.
These 8 rows form the pattern.

No. 4 Six Stitch Cable Back 10 sts.

1st row: (wrong side) K.2, p.6, k.2.
2nd row: P.2, k.6, p.2.
3rd row: As 1st row.
4th row: P.2, slip next 3 sts. to back on cable needle, k.3, then k.3 from cable needle, p.2.
5th to 8th rows: Repeat 1st and 2nd rows twice more.
These 8 rows form the pattern.

No. 5 Eight Stitch Cable Front 12 sts.

1st row: (wrong side) k.2, p.8, k.2.
2nd row: P.2, k.8, p.2.
3rd row: As 1st row.
4th row: P.2, slip next 4 sts. to front on cable needle, k.4, then k.4 from cable needle, p.2.
5th to 10th rows: Repeat 1st and 2nd rows 3 times.
These 10 rows form the pattern.

No. 6 Eight Stitch Cable Back 12 sts.

1st row: (wrong side) K.2, p.8, k.2.
2nd row: P.2, k.8, p.2.

10 *Six stitch cable front*

11 *Eight stitch cable back*

12 *Eight stitch cable front*

33

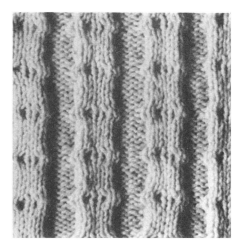

13 *Notched cable*

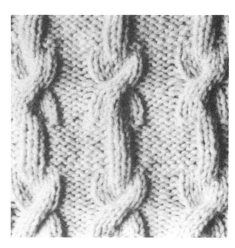

14 *Rib and cable cross*

15 *Figure eight cable pattern*

3rd row: As 1st row.

4th row: P.2, slip next 4 sts. to back on cable needle, k.4, then k.4 from cable needle, p.2.

5th to 10th rows: Repeat 1st and 2nd rows 3 times more. These 10 rows form the pattern.

No. 7 Notched Cable 11 sts.

A small and simple pattern, useful for fancy welts.

1st row: (wrong side) K.1, p.2, k.2, p.1, k.2, p.2, k.1.

2nd row: P.1, slip next 2 sts. to front on cable needle, p.2, then k.2. from cable needle, k.1, slip next 2 sts. to back on cable needle, k.2, then p.2 from cable needle, p.1.

3rd, 5th and 7th rows: K.3, p.5, k.3.

4th and 6th rows: P.3, k.5, p.3.

8th row: P.1, slip next 2 sts. to back on cable needle, k.2, then p.2 from cable needle, k.1, slip next 2 sts. to front on cable needle, p.2, then k.2 from cable needle, p.1.

These 8 rows form the pattern.

No. 8 Rib and Cable Cross 10 sts.

Suitable for allover patterns, this combination has wide rib and crossover cables.

1st, 3rd and 5th rows: P.2, k.6, p.2.

2nd, 4th and 6th rows: K.2, p.6, k.2.

7th row: P.2, slip next 3 sts. to back on cable needle, k.3, then k.3 from cable needle, p.2.

8th, 10th and 12th rows: As 2nd row.

9th and 11th rows: As 1st row.

13th, 15th, 17th and 19th rows: P.4, k.2, p.4.

14th, 16th, 18th and 20th rows: K.4, p.2, k.4.

These 20 rows form the pattern.

No. 9 Figure Eight Cable Pattern 12 sts.

Easy to work cable pattern against a background of reverse stocking stitch.

B.Cr., back cross thus: slip next st. to back on cable needle, k.2, then p.1 from cable needle.

F.Cr., front cross thus: slip next 2 sts. to front on cable needle, p.1, then k.2 from cable needle.

1st row: (wrong side) K.5, p.2, k.5.

2nd row: P.4, k.4, p.4.

3rd row and foll. alt. rows: K. the k. sts. and p. the p. sts. as they present themselves.

4th row: P.3, B.Cr., F.Cr., p.3.

6th row: P.2, B.Cr., p.2, F.Cr., p.2.

8th row: P.2, F.Cr., p.2, B.Cr., p.2.

10th row: P.3, F.Cr., B.Cr., p.3.

12th row: P.4, slip next 2 sts. to back on cable needle, k.2, then k.2 from cable needle, p.4.

14th row: As 4th row.

16th row: As 6th row.

18th row: As 8th row.

20th row: As 10th row.

21st row: K.4, p.4, k.4.

22nd, 24th and 26th rows: P.5, k.2, p.5.
23rd, 25th and 27th rows: K.5, p.2, k.5.
28th row: P.5, k.2, p.5.
These 28 rows form the pattern.

No. 10 Chain Link Knotted Cable 10 sts.
Knotted rib forms this traditional cable pattern.
1st row: (right side) (P.2, k.2) twice, p.2.
2nd row: (K.2, p.2) twice, k.2.
3rd row: P.2, slip next 4 sts. to front on cable needle, k.2, then slip the p.2 sts. from cable needle back on to left hand needle, pass the cable needle with remaining 2 sts. to back of work, p.2 from left hand needle, k.2 from cable needle, p.2.
4th, 6th and 8th rows: As 2nd row.
5th, 7th and 9th rows: As 1st row.
10th row: As 2nd row.
These 10 rows form the pattern.

No. 11 Cross Rib Cable 11 sts.
A frequently used cable pattern using twisted rib.
1st row: (wrong side) K.2, (p.1, k.1) 4 times, k.1.
2nd row: P.2, (k.1 t.b.l., p.1) 4 times, p.1.
3rd to 6th rows: Repeat 1st and 2nd rows twice more.
7th row: As 1st row.
8th row: P.2, slip next 4 sts. to front on cable needle, (k.1 t.b.l., p.1) twice from main needle, (k.1. t.b.l., p.1) twice from cable needle, p.1.
9th row: As 1st row.
10th and 11th rows: Repeat 2nd, then 1st rows.
12th row: As 2nd row.
These 12 rows form the pattern.

No. 12 Ribbed Cable Pattern 16 sts.
Stitches in reverse stocking stitch and single rib cross to make a chunky cable pattern with a garter stitch background.
1st row: (right side) K.2, (p.1, k.1) 3 times, p.6, k.2.
2nd, 4th and 6th rows: K.8, (p.1, k.1) 3 times, k.2.
3rd and 5th rows: As 1st row.
7th row: K.2, slip next 7 sts. to back on cable needle, p.5, from main needle, (p.2, k.1) 3 times, p.1 all from cable needle, k.2.
8th, 10th, 12th and 14th rows: K.3, (p.1, k.1) 3 times, k.7.
9th, 11th and 13th rows: K.2, p.6, (k.1, p.1) 3 times, k.2.
15th row: K.2, slip next 5 sts. to back on cable needle, (p.1, k.1) 3 times, p.1 all from main needle, p.5 from cable needle, k.2.
16th row: As 2nd row.
These 16 rows form the pattern.

No. 13 Coin or Shell pattern 12 sts.
It is easy to see how this cable, with its pretty shape, came by its name. When worked on fine needles it forms a close, well insulating fabric.
1st row: (wrong side) K.2, y.bk., slip 1, p.6, y.bk., slip 1, k.2.

16 *Chain link knotted cable*

17 *Cross rib cable*
18 *Ribbed cable pattern*

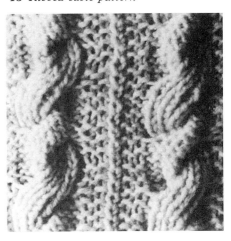

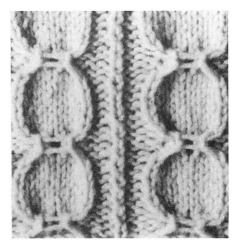

19 *Coin or shell pattern*

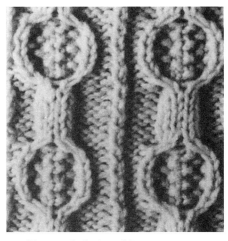

20 *Moss and chain cable*

21 *Wishbone pattern*

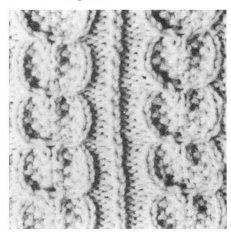

2nd row: P.2, slip next st. to front on cable needle, p.3, then k.1. from cable needle, slip next 3 sts. to back on cable needle, k.1, then p.3 from cable needle, p.2.
3rd row: K.5, p.2, k.5.
4th row: P.2, slip next 3 sts. to back on cable needle, k.1, then k.3 from cable needle, slip next st. to front on cable needle, k.3, then k.1. from cable needle, p.2.
5th, 7th and 9th rows: K.2, p.8, k.2.
6th, 8th and 10th rows: P.2, k.8, p.2.
These 10 rows form the pattern.

No. 14 Moss and Chain Cable 12 sts.
A pattern of moss stitch in a popular cable frame.
1st row: (wrong side) K.4, p.4, k.4.
2nd row: P.4, k.4, p.4.
3rd row: K.4, p.1, y.bk. slip 2, p.1, k.4.
4th row: P.2, slip next 3 sts. to back on cable needle, k.1, then p.1, k.1., p.1 all from cable needle, slip next st. to front on cable needle, k.1, p.1, k.1, then k.1 from cable needle, p.2.
5th, 7th and 9th rows: K.2, (p.1, k.1) 3 times, p.2, k.2.
6th, 8th and 10th rows: P.2, (k.1, p.1) 3 times, k.2, p.2.
11th row: K.2, y.bk. slip 1, (k.1, p.1) 3 times, y.bk. slip 1, k.2.
12th row: P.2, slip next st. to front on cable needle, p.2, k.1, then k.1 from cable needle, slip next 3 sts. to back on cable needle, k.1, then k.1, p.2 from cable needle, p.2.
13th, 14th, 15th and 16th rows: Repeat 1st and 2nd rows twice more.
These 16 rows form the pattern.

No. 15 Wishbone Pattern 12 sts.
Another moss stitch pattern, this time outlined by a wishbone cable.
1st row: (right side) P.2, slip next 3 sts. to back on cable needle, k.1, then p.1, k.1, p.1 from cable needle, slip next st. to front on cable needle, k.1, p.1, k.1, then k.1 from cable needle, p.2.
2nd, 4th and 6th rows: K.2, (p.1, k.1) 3 times, p.2, k.2.
3rd and 5th rows: P.2, (k.1, p.1) 3 times, k.2, p.2.
7th row: P.2, k.1, p.1, k.3, p.1, k.2, p.2.
8th row: K.2, p.1, k.1, p.3, k.1, p.2, k.2.
These 8 rows form the pattern.

No. 16 Heavy Cable with Bobbles 11 sts.
A rich cable pattern embossed with bobbles.
1st row: (wrong side) K.2, p.7, k.2.
2nd row: P.2, slip next 3 sts. to back on cable needle, k.4, then k.3 from cable needle, p.2.
3rd row and foll. alt. rows: As 1st row.
4th row: P.2, k.7, p.2.
6th row: As 4th row.
8th row: As 2nd row.
10th and 12th rows: As 4th row.
14th row: P.2, k.3, (k.1, y.fwd., k.1, y.fwd., k.1) all in next

st., turn and k.5, turn and p.5, turn and slip 1, k.1, p.s.s.o., k.1., k.2 tog., turn and p.3 tog.—bobble made, k.3, p.2.
16th row: As 4th row.
These 16 rows form the pattern.
Note: When working this cable pattern at both sides of a central panel, the cable may be reversed for the second repeat by working the 2nd row thus:
2nd row: P.2, slip next 4 sts. to front on cable needle, k.3, then k.4 from cable needle.

No. 17 Long Cable 12 sts.
This pattern draws its name from the long ribbed outer cable that surrounds the tiny inner cable pattern.
1st row: (wrong side) K.2, p.2 t.b.l., p.4, p.2 t.b.l., k.2.
2nd row: P.2, k.2 t.b.l., k.4, k.2 t.b.l., p.2.
3rd row and foll. alt. rows: As 1st row.
4th row: P.2, k.2 t.b.l., slip next 2 sts. to back on cable needle, k.2, then k.2 from cable needle, k.2 t.b.l., p.2.
6th row: As 2nd row.
8th row: As 2nd row.
10th row: P.2, slip next 4 sts. to back on cable needle, k.2, then k. the first 2 sts. from cable needle, bring the cable needle with the remaining 2 sts. through to front of work, k.2 from main needle, k.2 from cable needle, p.2.
These 10 rows form the pattern.

No. 18 Lobster Claw Cable 12 sts.
1st row: (wrong side) K.
2nd row: P.2, k.1, p.6, k.1, p.2.
3rd, 5th and 7th rows: K.2, p.2, k.4, p.2, k.2.
4th and 6th rows: P.2, k.2, p.4, k.2, p.2.
8th row: P.2, slip next 2 sts. to front on cable needle, p.2, y.fwd., k.2 tog. t.b.l. from cable needle, slip next 2 sts. to back on cable needle, k.2 tog., yarn round needle, p.2 from cable needle, p.2.
These 8 rows form the pattern.

No. 19 Aran Moss, Diamond and Bobble 17 sts.
Three of the truly traditional patterns combined to form a well balanced panel.
C. 3 B., cable 3 back thus: slip next st. to back on cable needle, k.2, then p.1 from cable needle.
C. 3 F., cable 3 front thus: slip next 2 sts. to front on cable needle, p.1, then k.2 from cable needle.
1st and 3rd rows: (wrong side) K.6, p.2, k.1, p.2, k.6.
2nd row: P.6, slip next 3 sts. to back on cable needle, k.2, then slip the p.1 from cable needle back on to the left hand needle and p. it, then k.2 from cable needle, p.6.
4th row: P.5, C. 3 B., k.1, C. 3 F., p.5.
5th row and foll. alt. rows: K. the k. sts. and p. the p. sts. as they present themselves.
6th row: P.4, C. 3 B., k.1, p.1, k.1, C. 3 F., p.4.
8th row: P.3, C. 3 B., (k.1, p.1) twice, k.1, C. 3 F., p.3.

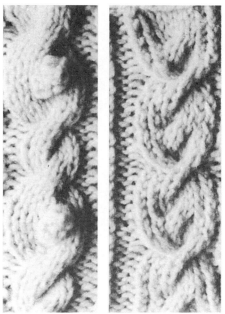

22 LEFT *Heavy cable with bobbles*

23 RIGHT *Long cable*

24 LEFT *Lobster claw cable*

25 RIGHT *Aran moss, diamond and bobble*

26 *Hourglass cable pattern*

27 *Aran diamond and rope pattern*

10th row: P.2, C. 3 B., (k.1, p.1) 3 times, k.1, C. 3 F., p.2.
12th row: P.2, C. 3 F., (p.1, k.1) 3 times, p.1, C. 3 B., p.2.
14th row: P.3, C. 3 F., (p.1, k.1) twice, p.1, C. 3 B., p.3.
16th row: P.4, C. 3 F., p.1, k.1, p.1, C. 3 B., p.4.
18th row: P.5, C. 3 F., p.1, C. 3 B., p.5.
20th row: As 2nd row.
22nd row: P.5, C. 3 B., p.1, C. 3 F., p.5.
24th row: P.4, C. 3 B., p.3, C. 3 F., p.4.
26th row: P.4, k.2, p.2, (k.1, y.fwd., k.1, y.fwd., k1) all in next st., turn and p. these 5 sts., turn and k.5, turn and p. 2 tog., p.1, p. 2 tog., turn and slip 1, k. 2 tog., p.s.s.o.—bobble made, p.2, k.2, p.4.
28th row: P.4, C. 3 F., p.3, C. 3 B., p.4.
30th row: As 18th row.
These 30 rows form the pattern.

No. 20 Hourglass Cable Pattern 14 sts.
An intricate series of twisting stitches form this elegant pattern.
B.Cr., back cross thus: slip next st. to back on cable needle, k.1 t.b.l., then p.1 from cable needle.
F.Cr., front cross thus: slip next st. to front on cable needle, p.1, then k.1 t.b.l. from cable needle.
1st row: (wrong side) K.4, p.1 t.b.l., k.1, p.2 t.b.l., k.1, p.1 t.b.l., k.4.
2nd row: P.3, (B.Cr.) twice, (F.Cr.) twice, p.3.
3rd row and foll. alt. rows: K. the k. sts. and p. the p. sts. as they present themselves.
4th row: P.2, B.Cr., slip next st. to back on cable needle, k.1 t.b.l., then k.1 t.b.l. from cable needle, p.2, slip next st. to front on cable needle, k.1 t.b.l., then k.1 t.b.l. from cable needle, F.Cr., p.2.
6th row: P.1, (B.Cr.) twice, F.Cr., B.Cr., (F.Cr.) twice, p.1.
8th row: (P.1, k.1 t.b.l.) twice, p.2, k.2 t.b.l., p.2, (k.1 t.b.l., p.1) twice.
10th row: P.1, (F.Cr.) twice, B.Cr., F.Cr., (B.Cr.) twice, p.1.
12th row: P.2, (F.Cr.) twice, p.2, (B.Cr.) twice, p.2.
14th row: P.3, (F.Cr.) twice, (B.Cr.) twice, p.3.
16th row: P.4, k.1 t.b.l., p.1, k.2 t.b.l., p.1, k.1 t.b.l., p.4.
These 16 rows form the pattern.

No. 21 Aran Diamond and Rope Pattern 18 sts.
A beautiful traditional pattern showing the rope cable entwined with the raised diamond.
C. 4, cable 4 thus: slip next 2 sts. to back on cable needle, k.2, then k.2 from cable needle.
C. 3 B., cable 3 back thus: slip next st. to back on cable needle, k.2, then p.1 from cable needle.
C. 3 F., cable 3 front thus: slip next 2 sts. to front on cable needle, p.1, then k.2 from cable needle.
1st row: (wrong side) K.7, p.4, k.7.
2nd row: P.6, slip next st. to back on cable needle, k.2, then k.1 from cable needle, slip next 2 sts. to front on cable

needle, k.1, then k.2 from cable needle, p.6.

3rd row and foll. alt. rows: K. the k. sts. and p. the p. sts. as they present themselves.

4th row: P.5, cable 3 sts. back as 2nd row, k.2, cable 3 sts. front as 2nd row, p.5.

6th row: P.4, C. 3 B., C. 4, C. 3 F., p.4.

8th row: P.3, C. 3 B., p.1, k.4, p.1, C. 3 F., p.3.

10th row: P.2, C. 3 B., p.2, C. 4, p.2, C. 3 F., p.2.

12th row: P.1, C. 3 B., p.3, k.4, p.3, C. 3 F., p.1.

14th row: P.1, k.2, p.4, C. 4, p.4, k.2, p.1.

16th row: P.1, C. 3 F., p.3, k.4, p.3, C. 3 B., p.1.

18th row: P.2, C. 3 F., p.2, C. 4, p.2, C. 3 B., p.2.

20th row: P.3, C. 3 F., p.1, k.4, p.1, C. 3 B., p.3.

22nd row: P.4, C. 3 F., C.4, C. 3 B., p.4.

24th row: P.5, C. 3 F., k.2., C. 3 B., p.5.

26th row: P.6, C 3 F., C. 3 B., p.6.

28th row: P.7, slip next 2 sts. to front on cable needle, k.2, then k.2 from cable needle, p.7.

These 28 rows form the pattern.

No. 22 Aran Diamond and Braid 16 sts.

A narrow panel of diamond, braid and rib that would make a neat centre panel for a sweater.

C. 4 B., cable 4 back thus: slip next 2 sts. to back on cable needle, k.2, then k.2 from cable needle.

C. 4 F., cable 4 front thus: slip next 2 sts. to front on cable needle, k.2, then k.2 from cable needle.

C. 3 B., cable 3 back thus: slip next st. to back on cable needle, k.2, then p.1 from cable needle.

C. 3 F., cable 3 front thus: slip next 2 sts. to front on cable needle, p.1, then k.2 from cable needle.

1st row: (wrong side) K.5, p.6, k.5.

2nd, 6th and 10th rows: P.5, k.2, C. 4 B., p.5.

3rd row and foll. alt. rows: K. the k. sts. and p. the p. sts. as they present themselves.

4th, 8th and 12th rows: P.5, C. 4 F., k.2, p.5.

14th row: P.4, C. 3 B., k.2, C. 3 F., p.4.

16th row: P.3, C. 3 B., p.1, k.2, p.1, C. 3 F., p.3.

18th row: P.2, C. 3 B., p.2, k.2, p.2, C. 3 F., p.2.

20th row: P.2, C. 3 F., p.2, k.2, p.2, C. 3 B., p.2.

22nd row: P.3, C. 3 F., p.1, k.2, p.1, C. 3 B., p.3.

24th row: P.4, C. 3 F., k.2, C. 3 B., p.4.

These 24 rows form the pattern.

No. 23 Simple Aran Braid 12 sts.

A simple method of producing a complex pattern, working the cable twist at alternating intervals on both sides of the centre.

C. 4 F., cable 4 front thus: slip next 2 sts. to front on cable needle, k.2, then k.2 from cable needle.

C. 4 B., cable 4 back thus: slip next 2 sts. to back on cable needle, k.2, then k.2 from cable needle.

1st row: (wrong side) K.2, p.8, k.2.

2nd row: P.2, k.4, C. 4 F., p.2.

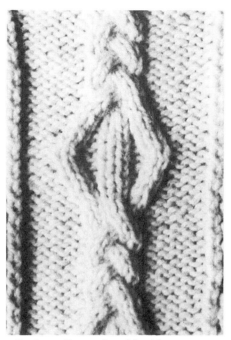

28 *Aran diamond and braid*

29 *Simple Aran braid*

30 LEFT *Five-fold Aran braid*

31 RIGHT *Twig plait cable*

32 LEFT *Wide plait cable*

33 RIGHT *Alternating plait cable*

3rd row and foll. alt. rows: As 1st row.
4th row: P.2, k.8, p.2.
6th row: As 2nd row.
8th row: P.2, C. 4 B., k.4, p.2.
10th row: As 4th row.
12th row: As 8th row.
These 12 rows form the pattern.

No. 24 Five-Fold Aran Braid 18 sts.

One form of the very old Aran braiding patterns, an intriguing plait of stitches that is surprisingly simple to work.
1st row: (wrong side) K.2, (p.2, k.1) 4 times, p.2, k.2.
2nd row: P.2, (k.2, p.1) 4 times, k.2, p.2.
3rd row and foll. alt. rows: As 1st row.
4th row: P.2, k.2, (p.1, slip next 3 sts. to front on cable needle, k.2, then slip the p. st. back on to left hand needle and p. it, then k. 2 from cable needle) twice, p.2.
6th row: As 2nd row.
8th row: P.2, (slip 3 sts. to back on cable needle, k.2, then slip the p. st. back on to left hand needle and p. it, then k.2 from cable needle, p.1) twice, k.2, p.2.
These 8 rows form the pattern.

No. 25 Twig Plait Cable 10 sts.

This attractive little pattern makes a good panel for outlining a centre panel.
1st row: (wrong side) K.2, p.6, k.2.
2nd row: P.2, slip next st. to front on cable needle, k.2, then k.1 from cable needle, slip next 2 sts. to back on cable needle, k.1, then k.2. from cable needle, p.2.
3rd row: As 1st row.
4th row: P.2, k.2, k. 2 tog. but do not slip loops off left hand needle, insert point of right hand needle between these 2 loop and k. a st. between them, then slip the loops off together, k.2, p.2.
These 4 rows form the pattern.

No. 26 Wide Plait Cable 12 sts.

Cabling the stitches in this pattern produces a chevron shape and not the rope typical of the previous samples.
B.Cr., back cross thus: slip next st. to back on cable needle, k.2, then k.1 from cable needle.
F.Cr., front cross thus: slip next 2 sts. to front on cable needle, k.1, then k.2 from cable needle.
1st row: (right side) P.4, slip next 2 sts. to back on cable needle, k.2, then k.2 from cable needle, p.4.
2nd row: K.4, p.4, k.4.
3rd row: P.3, B.Cr., F.Cr., p.3.
4th row: K.3, p.6, k.3.
5th row: P.2, B.Cr., k.2, F.Cr., p.2.
6th row: K.2, p.8, k.2.
7th row: P.1, B.Cr., k.4, F.Cr., p.1.
8th row: K.1, p.10, k.1.
These 8 rows form the pattern.

No. 27 Alternating Plait Cable 12 sts.

Beginners to cable designs would find this very old pattern easy to work.

1st row: (wrong side) K.3, p.6, k.3.

2nd row: P.3, k.6, p.3.

3rd row: As 1 st row.

4th row: P.3, slip next 2 sts. to back on cable needle, k.2, then k.2 from cable needle, k.2, p.3.

5th row: As 1st row.

6th row: P.3, k.2, slip next 2 sts. to front on cable needle, k.2, then k.2 from cable needle, p.3.

Repeat from 3rd to 6th rows for pattern.

No. 28 Simple Plait Cable 13 sts.

Another plaited cable for the novice; just two cable rows form the pattern.

1st row: (right side) P.2, k.9, p.2.

2nd row: K.2, p.9, k.2.

3rd row: P.2, slip next 3 sts. to front on cable needle, k.3, then k.3 from cable needle, k.3, p.2.

4th row: As 2nd row.

5th and 6th rows: As 1st and 2nd rows.

7th row: P.2, k.3, slip next 3 sts. to back on cable needle, k.3, then k.3 from cable needle, p.2.

8th row: As 2nd row.

These 8 rows form the pattern.

No. 29 Little Twist Plait 7 sts.

R.Tw., right twist thus: k. the second st. on left hand needle, then k. the first st. and slip both loops off together.

L.Tw., left twist thus: k. t.b.l. in second st. on left hand needle, then k. first and second sts. together t.b.l. and slip both loops off together.

1st and 3rd rows: (wrong side) K.2, p.3, k.2.

2nd row: P.2, R.Tw., k.1, p.2.

4th row: P.2, k.1, L.Tw., p.2.

These 4 rows form the pattern.

No. 30 Wide Twist Plait 10 sts.

A wider version of the previous twist plait.

R.Tw., right twist thus: k. the second st. on left hand needle, then k. first st. and slip both loops off together.

L.Tw., left twist thus: k. t.b.l. in second st. on left hand needle, then k. first and second sts. together t.b.l. and slip both loops off together.

1st and 3rd rows: (wrong side) K.3, p.5, k.2.

2nd row: P.2, k.3, R.Tw., p.3.

4th row: P.2, L.Tw., R.Tw., L.Tw., p.2.

5th and 7th rows: K.2, p.5, k.3.

6th row: P.3, L.Tw., k.3, p.2.

8th row: P.2, R.Tw., L.Tw., R.Tw., p.2.

These 8 rows form the pattern.

34 *Simple plait cable*

35 LEFT *Little twist plait*

36 RIGHT *Wide twist plait*

37 *Double twist braid*

38 LEFT *Cluster pattern braid*
39 RIGHT *Bobble pattern braid*

No. 31 Double Twist Braid 12 sts.
R.Tw., right twist thus: k. the second st. on left hand needle, then k. first st. and slip both loops off together.
L.Tw., left twist thus: k. t.b.l. in second st. on left hand needle, then k. first and second sts. together t.b.l. and slip both loops off together.
1st and 3rd rows: (wrong side) K.2, p.1, k.6, p.1, k.2.
2nd and 4th rows: P.2, k.1 t.b.l., p.6
k.1 t.b.l., p.2.
5th and 7th rows: K.2, p.1, k.2, p.2, k.2, p.1, k.2.
6th row: P.2, k.1 t.b.l., p.2, R.Tw., p.2, k.1 t.b.l., p.2.
8th row: P.2, (L.Tw., R.Tw.) twice, p.2.
9th and 11th rows: K.3, p.2, k.2, p.2, k.3.
10th row: P.3, R.Tw., p.2, L.Tw., p.3.
12th row: P.3, k.2, p.2, k.2, p.3.
13th to 19th rows: Repeat 9th to 12th rows, then 9th to 11th rows.
20th row: P.2, (R.Tw., L.Tw.) twice, p.2.
21st and 22nd rows: As 5th and 6th rows.
23rd to 26th rows: As 1st to 4th rows.
These 26 rows form the pattern.

No. 32 Cluster Pattern Braid 13 sts.
A braided pattern made more elaborate by the addition of clusters.
R.Tw., right twist thus: k. the second st. on left hand needle, then k. the first st. and slip both loops off together.
L.Tw., left twist thus: k. t.b.l. in second st. on left hand needle, then k. first and second sts. together t.b.l. and slip both loops off together.
1st row: (wrong side) K.3, p.1, k.1, p.2, k.2, p.1, k.3.
2nd row: P.3, L.Tw., p.1, L.Tw., R.Tw., p.3.
3rd row: K.4, p.2, k.2, p.1, k.4.
4th row: P.2 (k.1, y.fwd., k.1) all in next st., turn and p. these 3 sts., turn and k.3 wrapping yarn twice round needle for each k. st. (called begin cluster), p.1, L.Tw., p.1, R.Tw., p.4.
5th row: K.4, p.2, k.1, p.1, k.2, slip next 3 sts. dropping extra loops to make long sts. and slip these 3 long sts. back on to left hand needle, p. the 3 sts. tog. t.b.l. (cluster now completed), k.2.
6th row: P.2, L.Tw., p.1, k.1 t.b.l., R.Tw., L.Tw., p.3.
7th row: K.3, p.1, k.2, p.2, k.1, p.1, k.3.
8th row: P.3, L.Tw., R.Tw., p.1, R.Tw., p.3.
9th row: K.4, p.1, k.2, p.2, k.4.
10th row: P.4, L.Tw., p.1, k.1, R.Tw., begin cluster in next st., p.2.
11th row: K.2, complete cluster over next 3 sts., k.2, p.1, k.1, p.2, k.4.
12th row: P.3, R.Tw., L.Tw., k.1 t.b.l., p.1, R.Tw., p.2.
These 12 rows form the pattern.

No. 33 Bobble Pattern Braid 13 sts.
Another braid pattern with bobbles. These are worked more compactly than clusters.

R.Tw., right twist thus: k. the second st. on left hand needle, then k. first st. and slip both loops off together.
L.Tw., left twist thus: k. t.b.l. in second st. on left hand needle, then k. first and second sts. together t.b.l. and slip both loops off together.
M.B., make bobble thus: (k.1, y.fwd., k.1, y.fwd., k.1) all in next st., turn, k.5, turn, p.5, turn and k.1, slip 1, k. 2 tog., p.s.s.o., k.1., turn and p. 3 tog.—bobble made.
1st row and foll. alt. rows: (wrong side) P.
2nd row: K.2, L.Tw., k.2, R.Tw., k.5.
4th row: K.3, L.Tw., R.Tw., k.6.
6th row: K.4, L.Tw., k.4, M.B., k.2.
8th row: K.5, L.Tw., k.2, R.Tw., k.2.
10th row: K.6, L.Tw., R.Tw., k.3.
12th row: K.2, M.B., k.4, R.Tw., k.4.
These 12 rows form the pattern.

No. 34 Bobble and Wave Pattern 17 sts.

Bobbles enclosed in a wave pattern. Waves would be a natural choice for a fisherman's sweater.
C. 3 B., cable 3 back thus: slip 1 st. to back on cable needle, k.2, then p.1 from cable needle.
C. 3 F., cable 3 front thus: slip 2 sts. to front on cable needle, p.1, then k.2 from cable needle.
1st row: (wrong side) K.6, p.2, k.1, p.2, k.6.
2nd row: P.5, C. 3 B., p.1, C. 3 F., p.5.
3rd row and foll. alt. rows: K. the k. sts. and p. the p. sts. as they present themselves.
4th row: P.4, C. 3 B., p.3, C. 3 F., p.4.
6th row: P.4, k.2, p.2, (k.1, y.fwd., k.1, y.fwd., k.1) all in next st., turn and p.5, turn and k.5, turn and p. 2 tog., p.1, p. 2 tog., turn and slip 1, k. 2 tog., p.s.s.o.—bobble made, p.2, k.2, p.4.
8th row: P.4, C. 3 F., p.3, C. 3 B., p.4.
10th row: P.5, C. 3 F., p.1, C. 3 B., p.5.
12th row: As 2nd row.
14th row: As 4th row.
16th row: P.3, C. 3 B., p.5, C. 3 F., p.3.
18th row: P.2, C. 3 B., p.7, C. 3 F., p.2.
20th row: P.2, C. 3 F., p.7, C. 3 B., p.2.
22nd row: P.3, C. 3 F., p.5, C. 3 B., p.3.
24th and 26th rows: Repeat 8th, then 10th rows.
These 26 rows form the pattern.

No. 35 Bobble and Chevron Pattern 19 sts.

A richly textured panel set against a background of reverse stocking stitch. This pattern is also suitable for use as an allover pattern.
R. Tw., right twist thus: k. the second st. on left hand needle then k. first st. and slip both loops off together.
L.Tw., left twist thus: k. t.b.l. in second st. on left hand needle, then k. first and second sts. together t.b.l. and slip both loops off together.

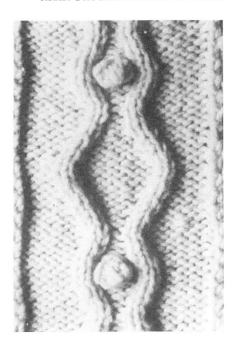

40 *Bobble and wave pattern*

41 *Bobble and chevron pattern*

43

1st row: (wrong side) K.6, (p.1, k.1) 4 times, k.5.

2nd row: P.5, (R.Tw.) twice, p.1, (L.Tw.) twice, p.5.

3rd row: K.5, (p.1, k.1) twice, k.2, (p.1, k.1) twice, k.4.

4th row: P.4, (R.Tw.) twice, p.3, (L.Tw.) twice, p.4.

5th row: K.4, (p.1, k.1) twice, k.4, (p.1, k.1) twice, k.3.

6th row: P.3, (R.Tw.) twice, p.5, (L.Tw.) twice, p.3.

7th row: K.2, (k.1, p.1) twice, k.7, (p.1, k.1) twice, k.2.

8th row: P.3, (k.1, y.fwd., k.1, y.fwd., k.1) all in next st., turn and p.5, turn and slip 1, k.1, p.s.s.o., k. 3 tog., pass the k. st. over the k. 3 tog.—bobble made (M.B.), p.1, L.Tw., p.5, R.Tw., p.1, M.B., p.3.

9th row: K.6, p.1, k.5, p.1, k.6.

10th row: P.6, L.Tw., p.3, R.Tw., p.6.

11th row: K.7, p.1, k.3, p.1, k.7.

12th row: P.7, M.B., p.3. M.B., p.7.

These 12 rows form the pattern.

No. 36 Chevron and Three-Bobble Pattern 21 sts.

A handsome panel of twist stitch chevrons and bobbles with garter stitch on reverse stocking stitch.

C. 4 B., cable 4 back thus: slip next st. to back on cable needle, k.1 t.b.l., p.1, k.1. t.b.l. all from main needle, then k.1. from cable needle.

C. 4 F., cable 4 front thus: slip next 3 sts. to front on cable needle, k.1, then k.1 t.b.l., p.1, k.1. t.b.l. all from cable needle.

M.B., make bobble thus: (k.1, y.fwd., k.1, y.fwd., k.1) all in next st., turn and p. 5, turn and k.3, k. 2 tog. then pass the k. 3 sts. over the k. 2 tog.—bobble made.

1st row: (wrong side) K.7, p.1, k.1, p.3, k.1, p.1, k.7.

2nd row: P.6, C. 4 B., k.1 t.b.l., C. 4 F., p.6.

3rd row: K.6, (p.1, k.1) 4 times, p.1, k.6.

4th row: P.5, C. 4 B., k.1, k.1 t.b.l., k.1, C. 4 F., p.5.

5th row: K.5, p.1, k.1, (p.1, k.2) twice, p.1, k.1, p.1, k.5.

6th row: P.4, C. 4 B., k.2, k.1 t.b.l., k.2, C. 4 F., p.4.

7th row: K.4, p.1, k.1, p.2, k.2, p.2, k.1, p.1, k.4.

8th row: P.3, C. 4 B., (k.1 t.b.l., k.2), twice, k.1 t.b.l., C. 4 F., p.3.

9th row: K.3, (p.1, k.1) twice, (p.1, k.2) twice, (p.1, k.1) twice, p.1, k.3.

10th row: P.2, C. 4 B., k.1, (k.1 t.b.l., k.2) twice, k.1 t.b.l., k.1, C. 4 F., p.2.

11th row: K.2, p.1, k.1, (p.1, k.2) 4 times, p.1, k.1, p.1, k.2.

12th row: P.1, C. 4 B., (k.2, k.1 t.b.l.) 3 times, k.2, C. 4 F., p.1.

13th row: (K.1, p.1) twice, k.3, (p.1, k.2) twice, p.1, k.3, (p.1, k.1) twice.

14th row: (P.1, k.1 t.b.l.) twice, k.3, (M.B., k.2) twice, M.B., k.3, (k.1 t.b.l., p.1) twice.

15th row: (K.1, p.1) twice, k.3, (p.1 t.b.l., k.2) twice, p.1 t.b.l., k.3, (p.1, k.1) twice.

16th row: (P.1, k.1 t.b.l.) twice, p.3, k.1 t.b.l., p.1, k.3 t.b.l., p.1, k.1 t.b.l., p.3, (k.1 t.b.l., p.1) twice.

These 16 rows form the pattern.

42 *Chevron and three-bobble pattern*

No. 37 Aran Diamonds with Popcorns 21 sts.
Popcorn in this sense is a term indicating a bobble type of stitch, but the diamond shape is traditional.
B.Cr., back cross thus: slip p. st. to back on cable needle, k.2, then p. st. from cable needle.
F.Cr., front cross thus: slip next 2 sts. to front on cable needle, p.1, then k.2 from cable needle.
1st row: (wrong side) P.2, k.3, k. in front, back, front, back and front of next st. (making 5 sts. out of 1) and slip the loop off left hand needle—popcorn begun, k.2, p.2, k.1, p.2, k.2, begin popcorn in next st., k.3, p.2.
2nd row: K.2, p.3, k.5 tog. t.b.l., (popcorn completed), p.2, slip next 3 sts. to front on cable needle, k.2, slip the p. st from cable needle back on to left hand needle and p. it, then k.2 from cable needle, p.2, k.5 tog. t.b.l., p.3, k.2.
3rd row: P.2, k.6, p.2, k.1, p.2, k.6, p.2.
4th row: K.2, p.5, B.Cr., p.1, F.Cr., p.5, k.2.
5th row: P.2, k.5, p.2, k.3, p.2, k.5, p.2.
6th row: K.2, p.4, B.Cr., p.3, F.Cr., p.4, k.2.
7th row: P.2, k.4, p.2, k.2, begin popcorn in next st, k.2, p.2, k.4, p.2.
8th row: K.2, p.3, B.Cr., p.2, k.5 tog. t.b.l. to complete popcorn, p.2, F.Cr., p.3, k.2.
9th row: P.2, k.3, p.2, k.7, p.2, k.3, p.2.
10th row: K.2, p.2, B.Cr., p.7, F.Cr., p.2, k.2.
11th row: P.2, k.2, p.2, k.2, begin popcorn in next st., k.3, begin popcorn in next st., k.2, p.2, k.2, p.2.
12th row: K.2, p.1, B.Cr., p.2, k.5 tog. t.b.l., to complete popcorn, p.3, k.5 tog. t.b.l., p.2, F.Cr., p.1, k.2.
13th row: P.2, k.1, p.2, k.11, p.2, k.1, p.2.
14th row: K.2, p.1, k.2, p.11, k.2, p.1, k.2.
15th row: P.2, k.1, p.2, k.3, begin popcorn in next st, k.3, begin popcorn in next st, k.3, p.2, k.1, p.2.
16th row: K.2, p.1, F.Cr., p.2, k.5 tog. t.b.l., to complete popcorn, p.3, k.5 tog. t.b.l., p.2, B.Cr., p.1, k.2.
17th row: P.2, k.2, p.2, k.9, p.2, k.2, p.2.
18th row: K.2, p.2, F.Cr., p.7, B.Cr., p.2, k.2.
19th row: P.2, k.3, p.2, k.3, begin popcorn in next st, k.3, p.2, k.3, p.2.
20th row: K.2, p.3, F.Cr., p.2, k.5 tog. t.b.l., to complete popcorn, p.2, B.Cr., p.3, k.2.
21st row: P.2, k.4, p.2, k.5, p.2, k.4, p.2.
22nd row: K.2, p.4, F.Cr., p.3, B.Cr., p.4, k.2.
23rd row: P.2, k.5, p.2, k.3, p.2, k.5, p.2.
24th row: K.2, p.5, F.Cr., p.1, B.Cr., p.5, k.2.
These 24 rows form the pattern.

No. 38 Allover Bobble Pattern 4 sts. plus 1
For those fascinated by bobbles, a pattern that is worked with bobbles all over a garter stitch background.
1st and 2nd rows: K.
3rd row: (right side) *K.3, (k. next st, do not remove loop made but place this new loop on left hand needle beside

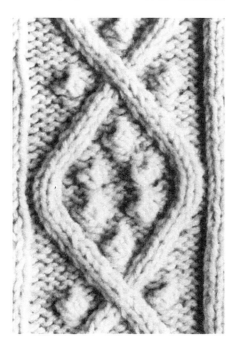

43 *Aran diamonds with popcorns*

44 *Allover bobble pattern*

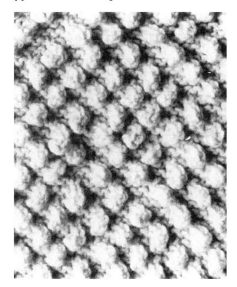

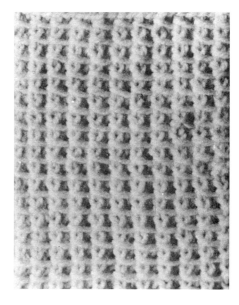

45 *Fancy welt rib*

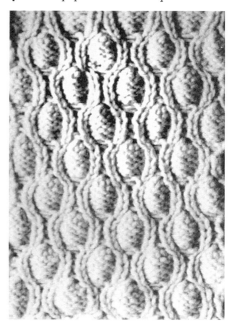

46 *Mock popcorn and cable pattern*

original st.) 4 times, now cast off these 4 sts. in the usual manner, the original st. will now be on the right hand needle; rep. from * to last st., k.1.

4th row: K.1, *p.1, k.3; rep. from * to end.

5th and 6th rows: K.

7th row: K.1, *cast on 4 sts. then cast off 4 sts. as 3rd row, k.3; rep. from * to end.

8th row: *K.3, p.1; rep. from * to last st., k.1.

These 8 rows form the pattern.

No. 39 Fancy Welt Rib Any even number of sts.

This unusual rib pattern is suitable for welts, cuffs and collars and also makes a useful texture for filling in between elaborate panels.

1st row: (wrong side) K.

2nd row: K.1, *P.2, then leaving yarn at front, slip these 2 sts. back on to left hand needle, pass yarn to back between needle points and slip the p.2 back on to right hand needle, bring yarn round needle, thus wrapping the p.2; rep. from * to last st, k.1.

These 2 rows form the pattern.

No. 40 Mock Popcorn and Cable Pattern 8 sts. plus 1

Although not a true Aran pattern, this panel provides an attractive fabric for all over use. The reverse side of the pattern is equally bold and adds another sample to the collection.

1st row: (wrong side) P.1, *k.1, p.1, k.5, p.1; rep. from * to end.

2nd row: K., *p.5, k.1, p.1, k.1; rep. from * to end.

3rd row: P.1, *pick up loop between sts. and k. into back of it—called k. loop inc., (k.1, p.1, k.1) all in next st., k. loop inc., p.1, p.5 tog., p.1.

4th, 6th and 8th rows: K.1, *p.1, k.1, p.5, k.1; rep. from * to end.

5th and 7th rows: P.1, *k.5, p.1, k.1, p.1; rep. from * to end.

9th row: P.1, *p.5 tog., p.1, k. loop inc., (k.1, p.1, k.1) all in next st., k. loop inc., p.1; rep. from * to end.

10th and 12th rows: As 2nd row.

11th row: As 1st row.

These 12 rows form the pattern.

No. 41 Irish Wave and Knot Pattern 14 sts. plus 5

Here is another method of producing bobbles, this time called knots. Combined with the wavy rib it forms a satisfactory allover pattern but may be used as a panel if required.

M.K., make knot thus: (k.1, p.1, k.1, p.1, k.1) all into next st. loosely, then, using point of left hand needle, pass the 2nd, 3rd, 4th and 5th sts. separately over the last st. made to complete the knot.

1st row: (wrong side) K.6, *p.2, k.1, p.1, k.1, p.2, k.7; rep. from * ending last rep., k.6.

2nd row: P.4, *p. 2 tog., k.2, p. twice in next st., k.1 t.b.l., p.

twice in next st., k.2, p.2 tog., p.3; rep. from * ending last rep., p.4.

3rd row: K.5, *p.2, k.2, p.1, k.2, p.2, k.5; rep. from * to end.

4th row: P.3, *p.2 tog., k.2, p. twice in next st., p.1, k.1 t.b.l., p.1, p. twice in next st., k.2, p.2 tog., p.1; rep. from * ending p.3.

5th row: K.4, *p.2, k.3, p.1, k.3, p.2, k.3; rep. from * ending last rep., k.4.

6th row: P.2, k.1 t.b.l., *p.1, k.2, p.3, M.K., p.3, k.2, p.1, k.1 t.b.l.; rep. from * ending last rep., p.2.

7th row: K.2, p.1, *k.1, p.2, k.7, p.2, k.1, p.1; rep. from * ending last rep., k.2.

8th row: P.2, k.1 t.b.l., *p. twice in next st., k.2, p. 2 tog., p.3, p.2 tog., k.2, p. twice in next st., k.1 t.b.l.; rep. from * ending last rep., p.2.

9th row: K.2, p.1, *k.2, p.2, k.5, p.2, k.2, p.1; rep. from * ending last rep., k.2.

10th row: P.2, k.1 t.b.l., *p.1, p. twice in next st., k.2, p.2 tog., p.1, p.2 tog., k.2, p. twice in next st., p.1, k.1 t.b.l.; rep. from * ending last rep., p.2.

11th row: K.2, p.1, *(k.3, p.2) twice, k.3, p.1; rep. from * ending last rep., k.2.

12th row: P.2, M.K., *p.3, k.2, p.1, k.1 t.b.l., p.1, k.2, p.3, M.K.; rep. from * ending last rep., p.2.

These 12 rows form the pattern.

No. 42 Waving Rib Pattern 13 sts. plus 1

Working the panel across the whole of the garment will produce an interesting raised texture.

L.Tw., left twist thus: k. the second st. on left hand needle, then k. first and second sts. together t.b.l. and slip both loops off together.

R.Tw., right twist thus: k. the second st. on left hand needle, then k. the first st. and slip both loops off together.

1st and 3rd rows (wrong side) P.2, *k.2, p.1, k.4, p.1, k.2, p.3; rep. from * ending last rep., p.2.

2nd row: K.2, *p.2, k.1, p.4, k.1, p.2, k.3; rep. from * ending last rep., k.2.

4th row: K.2, *p.2, L.Tw., p.2, R.Tw., p.2, k.3; rep. from * ending last rep., k.2.

5th row: P.2, *k.3, p.1, k.2, p.1, k.3, p.3; rep. from * ending last rep., p.2.

6th row: K.1, *L.Tw., p.2, L.Tw., R.Tw., p.2, R.Tw., k.1; rep. from * to end.

7th row: P.1, *k.1, p.1, k.3, p.2, k.3, p.1, k.1, p.1; rep. from * to end.

8th row: K.1, *p.1, L.Tw., (p.2, R.Tw.) twice, p.1, k.1; rep. from * to end.

9th row: P.1, *k.2, p.1, k.6, p.1, k.2, p.1; rep. from * to end.

10th row: K.1, *p.2, L.Tw., p.4, R.Tw., p.2, k.1; rep. from * to end.

11th and 13th rows: P.1, *k.3, p.1, k.4, p.1, k.3, p.1; rep. from * to end.

47 *Mock popcorn and cable pattern reversed*

48 *Irish wave and knot pattern*

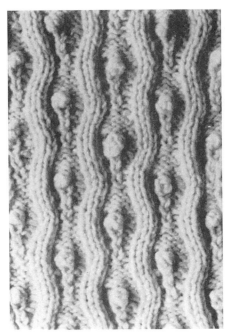

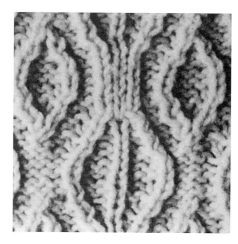

49 *Waving rib pattern*

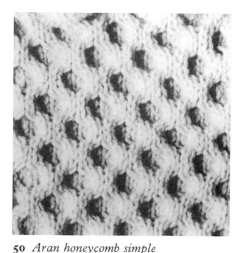

50 *Aran honeycomb simple*

51 *Aran honeycomb elongated*

12th row: K.1, *p.3, k.1, p.4, k.1, p.3, k.1; rep. from * to end.
14th row: K.1, *p.2, R.Tw., p.4, L.Tw., p.2, k.1; rep. from * to end.
15th row: P.1, *k.2, p.1, k.2, p.2, (k.2, p.1) twice; rep. from * to end.
16th row: K.1, *p.1, (R.Tw., p.2) twice, L.Tw., p.1, k.1; rep. from * to end.
17th and 19th rows: Repeat 7th then 5th rows.
18th row: K.1, *R.Tw., p.2, R.Tw., L.Tw., p.2, L.Tw., k.1; rep. from * to end.
20th row: K.2, *p.2, R.Tw., p.2, L.Tw., p.2, k.3; rep. from * ending last rep., k.2.
These 20 rows form the pattern.

No. 43 Aran Honeycomb Simple 8 sts.

A great favourite, this pattern is reminiscent of the shape of the honeycomb. It is suitable as a panel but also looks good when used as an allover fabric.
C. 4 B., cable 4 back thus: slip next 2 sts. to back on cable needle, k.2, then k.2 from cable needle.
C.4 F., cable 4 front thus: slip next 2 sts. to front on cable needle, k.2, then k.2 from cable needle.
1st row: (wrong side) P.
2nd row: C. 4 B., C. 4 F.
3rd row and foll. alt. rows: P.
4th row: K.
6th row: C. 4 F., C. 4 B.
8th row: K.
These 8 rows form the pattern.

No. 44 Aran Honeycomb Elongated 8 sts.

This is a bolder version of Aran honeycomb simple. Both of these patterns are very old and to be found amongst earliest knitting references.
C. 4 B., cable 4 back thus: slip next 2 sts. to back on cable needle, k.2, then k.2 from cable needle.
C. 4 F., cable 4 front thus: slip next 2 sts. to front on cable needle, k.2, then k.2 from cable needle.
1st row and foll. alt. rows: (wrong side) P.
2nd row: C. 4 B., C. 4 F.
4th and 6th rows: K.
8th row: C. 4 F., C. 4 B.
10th and 12th rows: K.
These 12 rows form the pattern.

No. 45 Broken Lattice Pattern Any multiple of 8 sts.

It is easy to see that this pattern may have been the result of an error in a normal lattice pattern. By missing a row of the diamond shape, this interesting allover pattern is formed.
L.Tw., left twist thus: k. t.b.l. in second st. on left hand needle, then k. first and second sts. together t.b.l. and slip both loops off together.
R.Tw., right twist thus: k. the second st. on left hand needle, then k. the first st. and slip both loops off together.

1st row and foll. alt. rows: (wrong side) P.
2nd row: L.Tw., k.2, L.Tw., R.Tw.
4th row: K.1, *L.Tw., k.2, R.Tw., k.2; rep. from * ending last rep., k.1.
6th row: R.Tw., L.Tw., R.Tw., k.2.
8th row: K.3, *L.Tw., k.2, R.Tw., k.2; rep. from * ending L.Tw., k.3.
These 8 rows form the pattern.

No. 46 Mock Cable Chevron 14 sts.

L. Tw., left twist thus: k. t.b.l. in second st. on left hand needle, then k. first and second sts. together t.b.l. and slip both loops off together.
R.Tw., right twist thus: k. the second st. on left hand needle, then k. the first st. and slip both loops off together.
1st row and foll. alt. rows: (wrong side) K.2, p.10, k.2.
2nd row: P.2, k.3, R.Tw., L.Tw., k.3, p.2.
4th row: P.2, k.2, R.Tw., k.2, L.Tw., k.2, p.2.
6th row: P.2, k.1, R.Tw., k.4, L.Tw., k.1, p.2.
8th row: P.2, R.Tw., k.6, L.Tw., p.2.
These 8 rows form the pattern.

No. 47 Tree of Life 15 sts.

This is a famous ancient pattern. It is said that the branches point to heaven when it is knitted in this way.
F.Cr., front cross thus: slip next st. to front on cable needle, p.1, then k.1 from cable needle.
B.Cr., back cross thus: slip next st. to back on cable needle, k.1, then p.1 from cable needle.
1st row: (right side) P.2, k.1, p.4, y.bk., slip 1, y.fwd., p.4, k.1, p.2.
2nd row: K.2, y.fwd., slip 1, y.bk., k.4, p.1, k.4, y.fwd. slip 1, y.bk., k.2.
3rd row: P.2, F.Cr., p.3, y.bk., slip 1, y.fwd., p.3, B.Cr., p.2.
4th row: K.3, y.fwd., slip 1, y.bk., k.3, p.1, k.3, y.fwd., slip 1, y.bk., k.3.
5th row: P.3, F.Cr., p.2, y.bk., slip 1, y.fwd., p.2, B.Cr., p.3.
6th row: K.4, y.fwd., slip 1, y.bk., k.2, p.1, k.2, y.fwd., slip 1, y.bk., k.4.
7th row: P.4, F.Cr., p.1, y.bk., slip 1, y.fwd., p.1, B.Cr., p.4.
8th row: K.5, y.fwd., slip 1, y.bk., k.1, p.1, k.1, y.fwd., slip 1, y.bk., k.5.
9th row: P.2, k.1, p.2, F.Cr., with yarn at back slip next st., B.Cr., p.2, k.1, p.2.
10th row: K.2, y.fwd., slip 1, y.bk., k.4, p.1, k.4, y.fwd., slip 1, y.bk., k.2.
Repeat 3rd to 10th rows for pattern.

No. 48 Twisted Tree of Life 9 sts.

With its uplifted branches, this pattern is thought by some to be the more authentic tree of life.
B.Cr., back cross thus: slip next st. to back on cable needle, k.1 t.b.l., then p.1 from cable needle.

52 *Broken lattice pattern*

53 *Mock cable chevron*
54 *Tree of life*

55 *Twisted tree of life*

56 *Double twist stitch reverse chevron*

F.Cr., front cross thus: slip next st. to front on cable needle, p.1, then k.1 t.b.l. from cable needle.

1st row: P.3, k.3 t.b.l., p.3.
2nd row: K.3, p.3 t.b.l., k.3.
3rd row: P.2, B.Cr., k.1 t.b.l., F.Cr., p.2.
4th row: K.2, (p.1 t.b.l., k.1) twice, p.1 t.b.l., k.2.
5th row: P.1, B.Cr., p.1, k.1 t.b.l., p.1, F.Cr., p.1.
6th row: K.1, (p.1 t.b.l., k.2) twice, p.1 t.b.l., k.1.
7th row: B.Cr., p.1, k.3 t.b.l., p.1, F.Cr.
8th row: P.1 t.b.l., k.2, p.3 t.b.l., k.2, p.1 t.b.l.
These 8 rows form the pattern.

No. 49 Double Twist Stitch Reverse Chevron 16 sts. plus 2

Chevrons are a recurring theme in Aran sweaters. These probably developed from the tree of life designs.
L.Tw., left twist thus: k. t.b.l. in second st. on left hand needle, then k. first and second sts. together t.b.l. and slip both loops off together.
R.Tw., right twist thus: K. the second st. on left hand needle then k. first st. and slip both loops off together.
1st row: (right side) P.1, k.1 t.b.l., *(L.Tw.) twice, p.6, (R.Tw.) twice, k.1 t.b.l., p.1; rep. from * to end.
2nd row: K.1, p.1, *k.1, p.3, k.6, p.3, k.1, p.1, k.1; rep. from * to end.
3rd row: P.1, k.1 t.b.l., *p.1, (L.Tw.) twice, p.4, (R.Tw.) twice, p.1, k.1 t.b.l., p.1; rep. from * to end.
4th row: K.1, p.1, *k.2, p.3, k.4, p.3, k.2, p.1, k.1; rep. from * to end.
5th row: P.1, k.1 t.b.l., *p.2, (L.Tw.) twice, p.2, (R.Tw.) twice, p.2, k.1 t.b.l., p.1; rep. from * to end.
6th row: K.1, p.1, *k.3, p.3, k.2, p.3, k.3, p.1, k.1; rep. from * to end.
7th row: P.1, k.1 t.b.l., *p.3, (L.Tw.) twice, (R.Tw.) twice, p.3, k.1 t.b.l., p.1; rep. from * to end.
8th row: K.1, p.1, *k.4, p.6, k.4, p.1, k.1; rep. from * to end.
9th row: P.1, k.1 t.b.l., *p.4, L.Tw., k.2, R.Tw., p.4, k.1 t.b.l., p.1; rep. from * to end.
10th row: K.1, p.1, *k.5, p.4, k.5, p.1, k.1; rep. from * to end.
11th row: P.1, k.1 t.b.l., *p.5, L.Tw., R.Tw., p.5, k.1 t.b.l., p.1; rep. from * to end.
12th row: K.1, p.1, *p.3, k.3, p.2, k.3, p.4, k.1; rep. from * to end.
These 12 rows form the pattern.

No. 50 Twisted Braid Chevrons 18 sts.

These chevrons with their anchor shapes stand out boldly against the smooth reverse stocking stitch background.
L.Tw., left twist thus: k. t.b.l. in second st. on left hand needle, then k. first and second sts. together t.b.l. and slip both loops off together.
R.T.w., right twist thus: k. second st. on left hand needle,

then k. first st. and slip both loops off together.

1st row: (wrong side) K.2, p.1 t.b.l., k.1, p.1, k.3, p.2, k.3, p.1, k.1, p.1 t.b.l., k.2.

2nd row: P.2, k.1 t.b.l., (R.Tw., p.3) twice, L.Tw., k.1 t.b.l., p.2.

3rd row: K.2, p.2, (k.4, p.2) twice, k.2.

4th row: P.2, R.Tw., p.3, R.Tw., L.Tw., p.3, L.Tw., p.2.

5th row: K.7, p.4, k.7.

6th row: P.6, R.Tw., k.2 t.b.l., L.Tw., p.6.

7th row: K.6, p.1, k.1, p.2 t.b.l., k.1, p.1, k.6.

8th row: P.5, R.Tw., p.1, k.2 t.b.l., p.1, L.Tw., p.5.

9th row: K.5, p.2, k.1, p.2 t.b.l., k.1, p.2, k.5.

10th row: P.4, R.Tw., k.1 t.b.l., p.1, k.2 t.b.l., p.1, k.1 t.b.l., L.Tw., p.4.

11th row: K.4, p.1, k.1, p.1 t.b.l., k.1, p.2 t.b.l., k.1, p.1 t.b.l., k.1, p.1, k.4.

12th row: P.3, R.Tw., p.1, k.1 t.b.l., p.1, k.2 t.b.l., p.1, k.1 t.b.l., p.1, L.Tw., p.3.

13th row: K.3, (p.2, k.1, p.1 t.b.l., k.1) twice, p.2, k.3.

14th row: P.2, R.Tw., k.1 t.b.l., p.1, k.1 t.b.l., R.Tw., L.Tw., k.1 t.b.l., p.1, k.1 t.b.l., L.Tw., p.2.

15th row: K.2, p.1, k.1, p.1 t.b.l., k.1, p.6, k.1, p.1 t.b.l., k.1, p.1, k.2.

16th row: P.2, (k.1 t.b.l., p.1) twice, R.Tw., k.2, L.Tw., (p.1, k.1 t.b.l.) twice, p.2.

17th row: K.2, (p.1 t.b.l., k.1) twice, p.1, k.1, p.2, k.1, p.1, (k.1, p.1 t.b.l.) twice, k.2.

18th row: P.2, k.1 t.b.l., p.1, k.1 t.b.l., (R.Tw., p.1) twice, L.Tw., k.1 t.b.l., p.1, k.1 t.b.l., p.2.

19th row: K.2, p.1 t.b.l., k.1, (p.2, k.2) twice, p.2, k.1, p.1 t.b.l., k.2.

20th row: P.2, k.1 t.b.l., p.1, R.Tw., p.2, k.2, p.2, L.Tw., p.1, k.1 t.b.l., p.2.

These 20 rows form the pattern.

No. 51 Simple Twist Stitch Reverse Chevron 14 sts.

R.Tw., right twist thus: K. second st. on left hand needle, then k. first st. and slip both loops off together.

L.Tw., left twist thus: k. t.b.l. in second st. on left hand needle, then k. the first and second sts. together t.b.l. and slip both loops off together.

1st row and foll. alt. rows: (wrong side) K.2, p.10, k.2.

2nd row: P.2, L.Tw., k.6, R.Tw., p.2.

4th row: P.2, k.1, L.Tw., k.4, R.Tw., k.1, p.2.

6th row: P.2, k.2, L.Tw., k.2, R.Tw., k.2, p.2.

8th row: P.2, k.3, L.Tw., R.Tw., k.3, p.2.

10th row: P.2, k.4, R.Tw., k.4, p.2.

These 10 rows form the pattern.

No. 52 Mock Tree of Life 14 sts.

This unobtrusive pattern follows the upward pointing branches of the traditional pattern but omits the twisted stitches, thus forming a pleasant overall pattern

57 *Twisted braid chevrons*

58 *Simple twist stitch reverse chevron*

59 *Mock tree of life*

60 *Crossover chevron and moss*

1st row: (right side) K.1, p.4, k.4, p.4, k.1.
2nd row and foll. alt. rows: K. the k. sts. and p. the p. sts. as they present themselves.
3rd row: K.1, p.3, k.6, p.3, k.1.
5th row: K.1, p.2, (k.2, p.1) twice, k.2, p.2, k.1.
7th row: K.1, p.1, (k.2, p.2) twice, k.2, p.1, k.1.
9th row: K.3, p.3, k.2, p.3, k.3.
11th row: K.2, (p.4, k.2) twice.
13th row: K.1, p.5, k.2, p.5, k.1.
14th row: As 2nd row.
These 14 rows form the pattern.

No. 53 Crossover Chevron and Moss 23 sts.
An elegant example of the embossed chevron with the classic Irish moss stitch in the centre.
B.Cr., back cross thus: slip next st. to back on cable needle, k.2, then p.1 from cable needle.
F.Cr., front cross thus: slip next 2 sts. to front on cable needle, p.1, then k.2 from cable needle.
1st and 3rd rows: (wrong side) K.2, p.1, k.1, k.5, p.2, k.1, p.2, k.5, p.1, k.1, p.1, k.2.
2nd row: P.2, k.1 t.b.l., p.1, p.5, slip next 3 sts. to back on cable needle, k.2, then slip p. st. from cable needle back on to left hand needle and p. it, then k. 2 from cable needle, p.5, p.1, k.1 t.b.l., p.2.
4th row: P.2, k.1 t.b.l., p.1, p.4, B.Cr., k.1, F.Cr., p.4, p.1, k.1 t.b.l., p.2.
5th row and foll. alt. rows: K. the k. sts. and p. the p. sts. as they present themselves.
6th row: P.2, k.1 t.b.l., p.1, p.3, B.Cr., k.1, p.1, k.1, F.Cr., p.3, p.1, k.1 t.b.l., p.2.
8th row: P.2, k.1 t.b.l., p.1, p.2, B.Cr., (k.1, p.1) twice, k.1, F.Cr., p.2, p.1, k.1 t.b.l., p.2.
10th row: P.2, k.1 t.b.l., p.1, p.1, B.Cr., (k.1, p.1) 3 times, k.1, F. Cr., p.1, p.1, k.1 t.b.l., p.2.
12th row: P.2, k.1 t.b.l., p.1, B.Cr., (k.1, p.1) 4 times, k.1, F.Cr., p.1, k.1 t.b.l., p.2.
14th row: P.2, k.1 t.b.l., p.1, k.2, p.3, k.2, p.1, k.2, p.3, k.2, p.1, k.1 t.b.l., p.2.
These 14 rows form the pattern.

No. 54 Single Leaf Twist Rib Diamond 19 sts.
The curves at the side edges of these diamonds form them into this graceful leaf shape.
R.Tw., right twist thus: k. the second st. on left hand needle, then k. the first st. and slip both loops off together.
L.Tw., left twist thus: K. t.b.l. the second st. on left hand needle, then k. first and second sts. together t.b.l. and slip both loops off together.
1st row: (wrong side) K.8, p.3, k.8.
2nd row: P.7, R.Tw., k.1, L.Tw., p.7.
3rd row: K.7, p.5, k.7.
4th row: P.6, R.Tw., k.3, L.Tw., p.6.

5th row: K.6, p.7, k.6.

6th row: P.5, (R.Tw.) twice, k.1 (L.Tw.) twice, p.5.

7th row: K.5, p.9, k.5.

8th row: P.4, (R.Tw.) twice, k.3, (L.Tw.) twice, p.4.

9th row: K.4, p.11, k.4.

10th row: P.3, (R.Tw.) 3 times, k.1, (L.Tw.) 3 times, p.3.

11th row: K.3, p.13, k.3.

12th row: P.2, (R.Tw.) 3 times, k.3, (L.Tw.) 3 times, p.2.

13th row: K.2, p.15, k.2.

14th row: P.2, k.1, (R.Tw.) 3 times, k.1, (L.Tw.) 3 times, k.1, p.2.

15th, 17th, 19th, 21st, 23rd and 25th rows: Repeat 13th, 11th, 9th, 7th, 5th and 3rd rows in that order.

16th row: P.2, L.Tw., (R.Tw.) twice, k.3, (L.Tw.) twice, R.Tw., p.2.

18th row: P.3, L.Tw., (R.Tw.) twice, k.1, (LTw.) twice, R.Tw., p.3.

20th row: P.4, L.Tw., R.Tw., k.3, L.Tw., R.Tw., p.4.

22nd row: P.5, L.Tw., R.Tw., k.1, L.Tw., R.Tw., p.5.

24th row: P.6, L.Tw., k.3, R.Tw., p.6.

26th row: P.7, L.Tw., k.1, R.Tw., p.7.

These 26 rows form the pattern.

No. 55 Twist Rib Diamond Leaves 16 sts. plus 1

This beautiful surface pattern is another variation of the diamond theme.

R.Tw., right twist thus: k. the second st. on left hand needle, then k. the first st. and slip both loops off together.

L.Tw., left twist thus: k. t.b.l. the second st. on left hand needle, then k. the first and second sts. together t.b.l. and slip both loops off together.

1st row and foll. alt. rows: (wrong side) P.

2nd row: K.1, *L.Tw., (R.Tw.) twice, k.3, (L.Tw.) twice, R.Tw., k.1; rep. from * to end.

4th row: K2, *L.Tw., (R.Tw.) twice, k.1, (L.Tw.) twice, R.Tw., k.3; rep. from * ending last rep., k.2.

6th row: K.1, *(L.Tw.) twice, R.Tw., k.3, L.Tw., (R.Tw.) twice, k.1; rep. from * to end.

8th row: K.2, *(L.Tw.) twice, R.Tw., k.1, L.Tw., (R.Tw.) twice, k.3; rep. from * ending last rep., k.2.

10th row: K1, *(L.Tw.) 3 times, k.3, (R.Tw.) 3 times, k.1; rep. from * to end.

12th row: K.2, *(L.Tw.) 3 times, k.1, (R.Tw.) 3 times, k.3; rep. from * to end.

14th, 16th, 18th, 20th and 22nd rows: Repeat 10th, 8th, 6th, 4th and 2nd rows in that order.

24th row: K.2, *(R.Tw.) 3 times, k.1, (L.Tw.) 3 times, k.3; rep. from * ending last rep., k.2.

26th row: K.1, *(R.Tw.) 3 times, k.3, (L.Tw.) 3 times, k.1; rep. from * to end.

28th row: As 24th row.

These 28 rows form the pattern.

61 *Single leaf twist rib diamond*

62 *Twist rib diamond leaves*

63 *Twist stitch diamonds*

64 *Aran diamond with twisted rib*

No. 56 Twist Stitch Diamonds 16 sts. plus 1
Unlike the raised Aran diamonds this brocade-like pattern does not draw in the knitted fabric.
R.Tw., right twist thus: k. the second st. on left hand needle, then k. the first st. and slip both loops off together.
L.Tw., left twist thus: k. t.b.l. the second st. on left hand needle, then k. first and second sts. together t.b.l. and slip both loops off together.
1st row and foll. alt. rows: P.
2nd row: K.1, *(L.Tw.) 3 times, k.3, (R.Tw.) 3 times, k.1; rep. from * to end.
4th row: K.2, *(L.Tw.) 3 times, k.1, (R.Tw.) 3 times, k.3; rep. from * ending last rep., k.2.
6th row and 8th row: As 2nd row and 4th row.
10th row: K.
12th row: K.2, *(R.Tw.) 3 times, k.1, (L.Tw.) 3 times, k.3; rep. from * ending last rep., k.2.
14th row: K1, *(R.Tw.) 3 times, k.3, (L.Tw.) 3 times, k.1; rep. from * to end.
16th row and 18th row: As 12th row and 14th row.
20th row: K.
These 20 rows form the pattern.

No. 57 Aran Diamond with Twisted Rib 16 sts. plus 1
This is a classic Aran diamond with twisted rib in place of the more common moss stitch.
B.Cr., back cross thus: slip next st. to back on cable needle, k.1 t.b.l., then p.1 from cable needle.
F.Cr., slip next st. to front on cable needle, p.1, then k.1 t.b.l. from cable needle.
1st row: (wrong side) K.1, *k.6, p.1, k.1, p.1, k.7; rep. from * to end.
2nd row: K.1, *p.6, slip next 2 sts. to front on cable needle, k.1 t.b.l. from main needle, slip the p. st. back on to left hand needle and p. it, then k.1 t.b.l. from cable needle, p.7; rep. from * to end.
3rd row: K.1, *k.6, p.1, k.1, p.1, k.7; rep. from * to end.
4th row: K.1, *p.5, B.Cr., k.1 t.b.l., F.Cr., p.6; rep. from * to end.
5th row and foll. alt. rows: K. the k. sts. and p. the p. sts. as they present themselves.
6th row: K.1, *p.4, B.Cr., p.1, k.1 t.b.l., p.1, F.Cr., p.5; rep. from * to end.
8th row: K.1, *p.3, B.Cr., (k.1 t.b.l., p.1) twice, k.1 t.b.l., F.Cr., p.4; rep. from * to end.
10th row: K.1, *p.2, B.Cr., (p.1, k.1 t.b.l.) 3 times, p.1, F.Cr., p.3; rep. from * to end.
12th row: K.1, *p.1, B.Cr., k.1 t.b.l., (p.1, k.1 t.b.l.) 4 times, F.Cr., p.2; rep. from * to end.
14th row: K.1, *p.1, F.Cr., k.1 t.b.l., (p.1, k.1 t.b.l.) 4 times, B.Cr., p.2; rep. from * to end.
16th row: K.1, *p.2, F.Cr., (p.1, k.1 t.b.l.) 3 times, p.1, B.Cr.,

p.3; rep. from * to end.

18th row: K.1, *p.3, F.Cr., (k.1 t.b.l., p.1) twice, k.1 t.b.l., B.Cr., p.4; rep. from * to end.

20th row: K.1, *p.4, F.Cr., p.1, k.1 t.b.l., p.1, B.Cr., p.5; rep. from * to end.

22nd row: K.1, *p.5, F.Cr., p.1, B.Cr., p.6; rep. from * to end.
These 22 rows form the pattern.

No. 58 Trellis with Moss Stitch 28 sts.

This is a very old Aran pattern; it may have represented the small fields within the dry stone walls or the moss that grew on the walls. It is frequently used as a centre panel.

F.Cr., front cross thus: slip next 2 sts. to front on cable needle, k.1, then k.2 from cable needle.

B.Cr., back cross thus: slip next st. to back on cable needle, k.2 t.b.l., then p.1 from cable needle.

F.Cr.P., front cross purl thus: slip next 2 sts. to front on cable needle, p.1, then k.2 t.b.l. from cable needle.

C.4 F., cable 4 front thus: slip next 2 sts. to front on cable needle, k.2 t.b.l., then k.2 t.b.l. from cable needle.

1st row: (right side) P.5, C.4 F., p.10, C.4 F., p.5.

2nd row and foll. alt. rows: K. the k. sts. and p. the p. sts. as they present themselves.

3rd row: P.4, B.Cr., F.Cr., p.8, B.Cr., F.Cr., p.4.

5th row: P.3, B.Cr., k.1, p.1, F.Cr., p.6, B.Cr., k.1, p.1, F.Cr., p.3.

7th row: P.2, B.Cr., (k.1, p.1) twice, F.Cr., p.4, B.Cr., (k.1, p.1) twice, F.Cr., p.2.

9th row: P.1, B.Cr., (k.1, p.1) 3 times, F.Cr., p.2, B.Cr., (k.1, p.1) 3 times, F.Cr., p.1.

11th row: *B.Cr., (k.1, p.1) 4 times, F.Cr.; rep. from * once more.

13th row: K. 2 t.b.l., (k.1, p.1) 5 times, C.4 F., (k.1, p.1) 5 times, k.2 t.b.l.

15th row: *F.Cr.P., (k.1, p.1) 4 times, B.Cr.; rep. from * once more.

17th row: P.1, F.Cr.P., (k.1, p.1) 3 times, B.Cr., p.2, F.Cr.P., (k.1, p.1) 3 times, B.Cr., p.1.

19th row: P.2, F.Cr.P., (k.1, p.1) twice, B.Cr., p.4, F.Cr.P., (k.1, p.1) twice, B.Cr., p.2.

21st row: P.3, F.Cr.P., k.1, p.1, B.Cr., p.6, F.Cr.P., k.1, p.1, B.Cr., p.3.

23rd row: P.4, F.Cr.P., B.Cr., p.8, F.Cr.P., B.Cr., p.4.

24th row: As 2nd row.
These 24 rows form the pattern.

65 *Trellis with moss stitch*

No. 59 Aran Diamonds with Moss Stitch 13 sts.

Another example of this old pattern, this one has a single twist stitch diamond surrounding the Irish moss pattern.

B.Cr., back cross thus: slip next st. to back on cable needle, k.1 t.b.l., then p.1 from cable needle.

F.Cr., front cross thus: slip next st. to front on cable needle, p.1, then k.1 t.b.l. from cable needle.

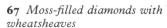

66 *Aran diamonds with moss stitch*

67 *Moss-filled diamonds with wheatsheaves*

1st row: (wrong side) K.5, p.1, k.1, p.1, k.5.
2nd row: P.5, slip next 2 sts. to front on cable needle, k.1. t.b.l., then slip the p. st. from cable needle back on to left hand needle and p. it, then k.1 t.b.l. from cable needle, p.5.
3rd row: As 1st row.
4th row: P.4, B.Cr., k.1, F.Cr., p.4.
5th row and foll. alt. rows: K. the k. sts. and p. the p. sts. as they present themselves.
6th row: P.3, B.Cr., k.1, p.1, k.1, F.Cr., p.3.
8th row: P.2, B.Cr., (k.1, p.1) twice, k.1, F.Cr., p.2.
10th row: P.1, B.Cr., (k.1, p.1) 3 times, k.1, F.Cr., p.1.
12th row: B.Cr., (k.1, p.1) 4 times, k.1, F.Cr.
14th row: F.Cr., (p.1, k.1) 4 times, p.1, B.Cr.
16th row: P.1, F.Cr., (p.1, k.1) 3 times, p.1, B.Cr., p.1.
18th row: P.2, F.Cr., (p.1, k.1) twice, p.1, B.Cr., p.2.
20th row: P.3, F.Cr., p.1, k.1, p.1, B.Cr., p.3.
22nd row: P.4, F.Cr., p.1, B.Cr., p.4.
These 22 rows form the pattern.

No. 60 Moss-filled Diamonds and Wheatsheaves 29 sts.
An attractive representational sample suitable for a sweater centre panel.
K. loop inc., knit loop increase thus: pick up loop lying between sts. and k. in back of it.
1st row: (right side) (P.2, k.2) 3 times, p.2, k. loop inc., p.1, k. loop inc., p.2, (k.2, p.2) 3 times.
2nd row: (K.2, p.2) 3 times, k.2, p.1, k.1, p.1, k.2, (p.2, k.2) 3 times
3rd row: (P.2, k.2) 3 times, p.2, k. loop inc., p.1, k.1, p.1, k. loop inc., p.2, (k.2, p.2) 3 times.
4th row: (K.2, p.2) 3 times, k.2, (p.1, k.1) twice, p.1, k.2, (p.2, k.2) 3 times.
5th row: (P.2, k.2) 3 times, p.2, k. loop inc., (p.1, k.1) twice, p.1, k. loop inc., p.2, (k.2, p.2) 3 times.
6th row: (K.2, p.2) 3 times, k.2, (p.1, k.1) 3 times, p.1, k.2, (p.2, k.2) 3 times.
7th row: (P.2, k.2) 3 times, p.2, k. loop inc., (p.1, k.1) 3 times, p.1, k. loop inc., p.2, (k.2, p.2) 3 times.
8th row: (K.2, p.2) 3 times, k.2, (p.1, k.1) 4 times, p.1, k.2, (p.2, k.2) 3 times.
9th row: (P.2, k.2) 3 times, p.2, k. loop inc., (p.1, k.1) 4 times, p.1, k. loop inc., p.2, (k.2, p.2) 3 times.
10th row: K.1, k. twice in next st., then with yarn to wrong side, slip the next 10 sts., pass the first of these slipped sts. over the other 9 sts. k.2, (p.1, k.1) 5 times, p.1, k.1, k. twice in next st., slip 10 sts., pass first st. over the other 9 sts., k.2.
11th row: (P.2, k.2) 3 times, p.2, slip 1, k.1, p.s.s.o., (p.1, k.1) 3 times, p.1, k. 2 tog., p.2, (k.2, p.2) 3 times.
12th row: (K.2, p.2) 3 times, k.2, (p.1, k.1) 4 times, p.1, k.2, (p.2, k.2) 3 times.
13th row: (P.2, k.2) 3 times, p.2, slip 1, k.1, p.s.s.o., (p.1, k.1) twice, p.1, k. 2 tog., p.2, (k.2, p.2) 3 times.

14th row: (K.2, p.2) 3 times, k.2, (p.1, k.1) 3 times, p.1, k.2, (p.2, k.2) 3 times.

15th row: (P.2, k.2) 3 times, p.2, slip 1, k.1, p.s.s.o., p.1, k.1, p.1, k. 2 tog., p.2, (k.2, p.2) 3 times.

16th row: (K.2, p.2) 3 times, k.2, (p.1, k.1) twice, p.1, k.2, (p.2, k.2) 3 times.

17th row: (P.2, k.2) 3 times, p.2, slip 1, k.1, p.s.s.o., p.1, k. 2 tog., p.2, (k.2, p.2) 3 times.

18th row: (K.2, p.2) 3 times, k.2, p.1, k.1, p.1, k.2, (p.2, k.2) 3 times.

19th row: (P.2, k.2) 3 times, p.2, slip 1, k. 2 tog., p.s.s.o., p.2, (k.2, p.2) 3 times.

20th row: (K.2, p.2) 3 times, k.2, p.1, k.2, (p.2, k.2) 3 times.

These 20 rows form the pattern.

No. 61 Mock Aran Diamonds 29 sts.

A smooth version of diamonds omits the need for cable and twisted stitches.

1st row: (right side) K.1, p.12, k.3, p.12, k.1

2nd row and foll. alt. rows: K. the k. sts. and p. the p. sts. as they present themselves.

3rd row: K.1, p.11, k.5, p.11, k.1.

5th row: K.1, p.10, k.3, p.1, k.3, p.10, k.1.

7th row: K.1, p.9, k.3, p.1, k.1, p.1, k.3, p.9, k.1.

9th row: K.1, p.8, k.3, (p.1, k.1) twice, p.1, k.3, p.8, k.1.

11th row: K.1, p.7, k.3, (p.1, k.1) 3 times, p.1, k.3, p.7, k.1.

13th row: K.1, p.6, k.3, (p.1, k.1) 4 times, p.1, k.3, p.6, k.1.

15th and 16th rows: As 11th and 12th rows.

17th and 18th rows: As 9th and 10th rows.

19th and 20th rows: As 7th and 8th rows.

21st and 22nd rows: As 5th and 6th rows.

23rd and 24th rows: As 3rd and 4th rows.

These 24 rows form the pattern.

No. 62 Rib Trellis on Reverse Stocking Stitch Background 18 sts. plus 6

C. 6 B., cable 6 back thus: slip next 3 sts. to back on cable needle, k.3, then k.3 from cable needle.

C. 6 B.P., cable 6 back purl thus: slip next 3 sts. to back on cable needle, k.3, then p.3 from cable needle.

C. 6 F.P., cable 6 front purl thus: slip next 3 sts. to front on cable needle, p.3, then k.3 from cable needle.

C. 6 F., cable 6 front thus: slip next 3 sts. to front on cable needle, k.3, then k.3 from cable needle.

1st row: (right side) P.9, *k.6, p.12; rep. from * to last 15 sts., k.6, p.9.

2nd row: K.9, *p.6, k.12; rep. from * to last 15 sts., p.6, k.9.

3rd row: P.9, *C. 6 B., p.12; rep from * ending last rep., p.9.

4th, 6th and 8th rows: As 2nd row.

5th and 7th rows: P.9, *k.6, p.12; rep from * ending last rep., p.9.

9th row: P.6, *C. 6 B.P., C. 6 F.P., p.6; rep from * to end.

10th, 12th and 14th rows: K.6, *p.3, k.6; rep. from * ending

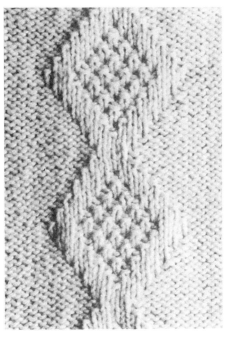

68 *Mock Aran diamonds*

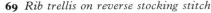

69 *Rib trellis on reverse stocking stitch*

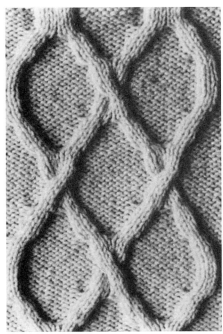

last rep., k.6.

11th and 13th rows: P.6, *k.3, p.6; rep from * to end.

15th row: P.3, *C. 6 B.P., p.6, C. 6 F.P.; rep from * to last 3 sts., p.3.

16th, 18th and 20th rows: K.3, p.3, *k.12, p.6; rep from * ending last rep., p.3, k.3.

17th and 19th rows: P.3, k.3, *p.12, k.6; rep. from * ending last rep., k.3, p.3.

21st row: P.3, k.3, *p.12, C. 6 F.; rep. from * ending last rep., k.3, p.3.

22nd, 24th and 26th rows: K.3, p.3, *k.12, p.6; rep. from * ending p.3, k.3.

23rd and 25th rows: P.3, k.3, *p.12, k.6; rep. from * ending last rep., k.3, p.3.

27th row: P.3, *C. 6 F.P., p.6, C. 6 B.P..; rep. from * ending p.3.

28th, 30th and 32nd rows: K.6, *p.3, k.6; rep. from * to end.

29th and 31st rows: P.6, *k.3, p.6; rep. from * to end.

33rd row: P.6, * C. 6 F.P., C. 6 B.P., p.6; rep. from * to end.

34th, 36th and 38th rows: K.9, *p.6, k.12; rep. from * ending last rep., k.9.

35th and 37th rows: P.9, *k.6, p.12; rep. from * ending last rep., p.9.

Repeat 3rd to 38th rows for pattern.

No. 63 Figure Eight Diamond Pattern 22 sts.

B.Cr., back cross thus: slip next st. to back on cable needle, k.2, then p.1 from cable needle.

F.Cr., front cross thus: slip next 2 sts. to front on cable needle, p.1, then k.2 from cable needle.

C. 4 B., cable 4 back thus: slip next 2 sts. to back on cable needle, k.2, then k.2 from cable needle.

1st row: (wrong side) K.9, p.4, k.9.

2nd row: P.9, C. 4 B., p.9.

3rd row and foll. alt. rows: K. the k. sts. and p. the p. sts. as they present themselves.

4th row: P.8, B.Cr., F.Cr., p.8.

6th row: P.7, B.Cr., p.2, F.Cr., p.7.

8th row: P.6, B.Cr., p.4, F.Cr., p.6.

10th row: P.5, B.Cr., p.1, k.4, p.1, F.Cr., p.5.

12th row: P.4, B.Cr., p.1, B.Cr., F.Cr., p.1, F.Cr., p.4.

14th row: P.3, B.Cr., p.1., B.Cr., p.2, F.Cr., p.1, F.Cr., p.3.

16th row: (P.2, B.Cr., p.2, F.C.r.) twice, p.2.

18th row: P.1, (B.Cr., p.4, F.Cr.) twice, p.1.

20th row: P.1, k.2, p.6, C. 4 B., p.6, k.2, p.1.

22nd row: P.1, (F.Cr., p.4, B.Cr.) twice, p.1.

24th row: (P.2, F.Cr., p.2, B.Cr.) twice, p.2.

26th row: P.3, F.Cr., p.1, F.Cr., p.2, B.Cr., p.1, B.Cr., p.3.

28th row: P.4, F.Cr., p.1, F.Cr., B.Cr., p.1, B.Cr., p.4.

30th row: P.5, F.Cr., p.6, B.Cr., p.5.

32nd row: P.6, F.Cr., p.4., B.Cr., p.6.

34th row: P.7. F.Cr., p.2, B.Cr., p.7.

70 *Figure eight diamond pattern*

36th row: P.8, F.Cr., B.Cr., p.8.
These 36 rows form the pattern.

No. 64 Mock Aran Marriage Lines 7 sts.
A useful narrow panel suitable for filling between broad patterns, as a centre panel or for an allover fabric.
1st row: (right side) P.1, k.1, p.1, k.4.
2nd row and foll. alt. rows: K. the k. sts. and p. the p. sts. as they present themselves.
3rd row: (K.1, p.1) twice, k.3.
5th row: K.2, p.1, k.1, p.1, k.2.
7th row: K.3, (p.1, k.1) twice.
9th row: K.4, p.1, k.1, p.1.
11th and 12th rows: As 7th and 8th rows.
13th and 14th rows: As 5th and 6th rows.
15th and 16th rows: As 3rd and 4th rows.
These 16 rows form the pattern.
Note: When two of these zigzag panels are worked, one on each side of a central panel, begin one pattern on 1st row and the other on 9th row to reverse the direction.

No. 65 Twist Stitch Zigzag Wavy Lines 10 sts.
R.Tw., right twist thus: K. second st. on left hand needle, p. the first st. and slip both loops off together.
L.Tw., left twist thus: P. in back of second st. on left hand needle, k. the first st. and slip both loops off together.
1st row: (wrong side) K.6, (p.1, k.1) twice.
2nd row: (L.Tw.) twice, p.6.
3rd row: K.6, (p.1, k.1) twice.
4th row: P.1, (L.Tw.) twice, p.5.
5th row: K.5, (p.1, k.1) twice, k.1.
6th row: P.2, (L.Tw.) twice, p.4
7th row: K.4, (p.1, k.1) twice, k.2.
8th row: P.3, (L.Tw.) twice, p.3.
9th row: K.3, (p.1, k.1) twice, k.3.
10th row: P.4, (L.Tw.) twice, p.2.
11th row: K.2, (p.1, k.1) twice, k.4.
12th row: P.5, (L.Tw.) twice, p.1.
13th row: (K.1, p.1) twice, k.6.
14th row: P.6, (L.Tw.) twice.
15th row: (P.1, k.1) twice, k.6.
16th row: P.6, (p.1, k.1) twice.
17th, 19th, 21st, 23rd, 25th, 27th, 29th and 31st rows: As 15th, 13th, 11th, 9th, 7th, 5th, 3rd and 1st rows in that order.
18th row: P.6, (R.Tw.) twice.
20th row: P.5, (R.Tw.) twice, p.1.
22nd row: P.4, (R.Tw.) twice, p.2.
24th row: P.3, (R.Tw.) twice, p.3.
26th row: P.2, (R.Tw.) twice, p.4.
28th row: P.1, (R.Tw.) twice, p.5.
30th row: (R.Tw.) twice, p.6.
32nd row: (K.1, p.1) twice, p.6.
These 32 rows form the pattern.

71 *Mock Aran marriage lines*

72 *Twist stitch zigzag wavy lines*

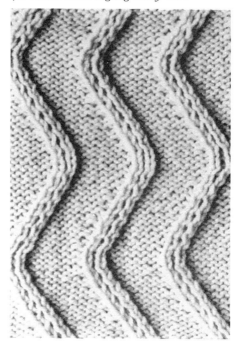

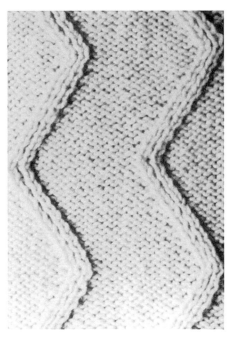

73 *Zigzag pattern with sharp outline*

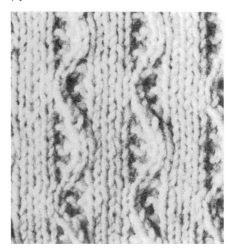

74 *Wave welt rib*

No. 66 Zigzag Pattern with Sharp Outline 15 sts.

B.Cr., back cross thus: slip next st. to back on cable needle, k.1, then p.1 from cable needle.

F.Cr., front cross thus: slip next st. to front on cable needle, p.1, then k.1 from cable needle.

1st row: (wrong side) K.2, p.1, k.1, p.1, k.10.
2nd row: P.9, (B.Cr.) twice, p.2.
3rd row: K.3, p.1, k.1, p.1, k.9.
4th row: P.8, (B.Cr.) twice, p.3.
5th row and foll. alt. rows: K. the k. sts. and p. the p. sts. as they present themselves.
6th row: P.7, (B.Cr.) twice, p.4.
8th row: P.6, (B.Cr.) twice, p.5.
10th row: P.5, (B.Cr.) twice, p.6.
12th row: P.4, (B.Cr.) twice, p.7.
14th row: P.3, (B.Cr.) twice, p.8.
16th row: P.2, (B.Cr.) twice, p.9.
18th row: P.2, (F.Cr.) twice, p.9.
20th row: P.3, (F.Cr.) twice, p.8.
22nd row: P.4, (F.Cr.) twice, p.7.
24th row: P.5, (F.Cr.) twice, p.6.
26th row: P.6, (F.Cr.) twice, p.5.
28th row: P.7, (F.Cr.) twice, p.4.
30th row: P.8, (F.Cr.) twice, p.3.
32nd row: P.9, (F.Cr.) twice, p.2.
These 32 rows form the pattern.

No. 67 Wave Welt Rib 6 sts. plus 1

L.Tw., left twist thus: k. t.b.l. the second st. on left hand needle, the k. first and second sts. together t.b.l. and slip both loops off together.

R.Tw., right twist thus: k. second st. on left hand needle, then k. first st. and slip both loops off together.

1st row: (right side) K.
2nd row: P.2, *k.2, p.4; rep. from * ending last rep., p.3.
3rd row: K.2, *L.Tw., k.4; rep. from * ending L.Tw., k.3.
4th row: P.2, *k.1, p.1, k.1, p.3; rep. from * ending last rep., p.2.
5th row: K.3, *L.Tw., k.4; rep. from * ending L.Tw., k.2.
6th row: P.3, *k.2, p.4; rep. from * ending k.2, p.2.
7th row: K.
8th row and 10th row: Repeat 6th row and 4th row.
9th row: K.3, *R.Tw., k.4; rep. from * ending R.Tw., k.2.
11th row: K.2, *R.Tw., k.4; rep. from * ending R.Tw., k.3.
12th row: As 2nd row.
These 12 rows form the pattern.

No. 68 Twigs and Rib Welt Pattern 8 sts. plus 4.

L.Tw., left twist thus: k. t.b.l. second st. on left hand needle, then k. first and second sts. together t.b.l. and slip both loops off together.

R.Tw., right twist thus: k. second st. on left hand needle, then k. first st. and slip both loops off together.

1st row: (wrong side) K.1, p.3, *k.5, p.3; rep. from * to end.
2nd row: *L.Tw., k.1, p.5; rep. from * ending L.Tw., k.1, p.1.
3rd and 5th rows: As 1st row.
4th row: *K.1, L.Tw., p.5; rep. from * ending k.1, L.Tw., p.1.
6th row: P.1, *k.2, p.4, R.Tw.; rep. from * ending k.2, p.1.
7th row: K.1, *p.2, k.1, p.1, k.4; rep. from * ending p.2, k.1.
8th row: P.1, *k.2, p.3, R.Tw., p.1; rep. from * ending k.2, p.1.
9th row: K.1, *p.2, k.2, p.1, k.3; rep. from * ending p.2, k.1.
10th row: P.1, *k.2, p.2, R.Tw., p.2; rep. from * ending k.2, p.1.
11th row: K.1, *p.2, k.3, p.1, k.2; rep. from * ending p.2, k.1.
12th row: P.1, *k.2, p.1, R.Tw., p.3; rep. from * ending k.2, p.1.
13th row: K.1, *p.2, k.4, p.1, k.1; rep. from * ending p.2, k.1.
14th row: P.1, *k.2, R.Tw., p.4; rep. from * ending k.2, p.1.
15th row: *P.3, k.5; rep. from * ending p.3, k.1.
16th row: P.1, *k.1, R.Tw., p.5; rep. from * ending k.1, R.Tw.
17th and 19th rows: As 15th row.
18th row: P.1, *R.Tw., k.1, p.5; rep. from * ending R.Tw., p.1.
20th row: P.1, *k.2, L.Tw., p.4; rep. from * ending k.2, p.1.
21st, 23rd, 25th and 27th rows: Repeat 13th, 11th, 9th and 7th rows in that order.
22nd row: P.1, *k.2, p.1, L.Tw., p.3; rep. from * ending k.2, p.1.
24th row: P.1, *k.2, p.2, L.Tw., p.2; rep. from * ending k.2, p.1.
26th row: P.1, *k.2, p.3, L.Tw., p.1; rep. from * ending k.2, p.1.
28th row: P.1, *k.2, p.4, L.Tw.; rep. from * ending k.2, p.1.
These 28 rows form the pattern.

No. 69 Rib with Small Twist Stitch Cable Welt Pattern 8 sts. plus 3

Traditional fishing shirts have very deep welts, sometimes termed skirts, and these are always worked in small patterns with rib instead of the usual rib, although rib is often used for the collar and cuffs. This pattern and the previous two patterns are typical examples.
1st row: (right side) *K.3, p.1, k.1 t.b.l., p.1, k.1 t.b.l., p.1; rep. from * to last 3 sts., k.3.
2nd row: P.3, *k.1, p.1 t.b.l., k.1, p.1 t.b.l., p.3, k.1; rep. from * to end.
3rd to 6th rows: As 1st and 2nd rows.
7th row: *K.3, p.1, slip next 2 sts. to front on cable needle, k.1 t.b.l., then p.1, k.1. t.b.l. from cable needle, p.1; rep. from * to last 3 sts., k.3.
8th row: As 2nd row.
These 8 rows form the pattern.

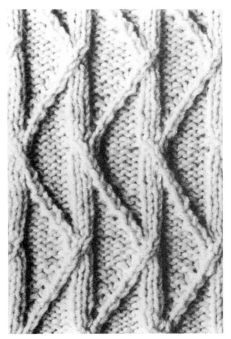

75 *Twig and rib welt pattern*

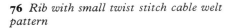

76 *Rib with small twist stitch cable welt pattern*

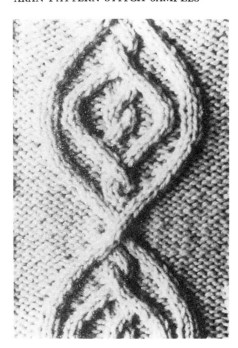

77 Triple cable pattern

No. 70 **Triple Cable Pattern** 26 sts.

A beautiful centre panel with three sets of twining cables.

C. 4 B., cable 4 back thus: slip next 2 sts. to back on cable needle, k.2, then k.2 from cable needle.

C. 4 F., cable 4 front thus: slip next 2 sts. to front on cable needle, k.2, then k.2 from cable needle.

C. 4 B.P., cable 4 back purl thus: slip next 2 sts. to back on cable needle, k.2, then p.2 from cable needle.

C. 4 F.P., cable 4 front purl thus: slip next 2 sts. to front on cable needle, p.2, then k.2 from cable needle.

B.Cr., back cross thus: slip next st. to back on cable needle, k.2, then p.1 from cable needle.

F.Cr., front cross thus: slip next 2 sts. to front on cable needle, p.1, then k.2 from cable needle.

1st and 3rd rows: (wrong side) K.11, p.4, k.11.

2nd row: P.11, C. 4 B., p.11.

4th row: P.9, C. 4 B., C. 4 F., p.9.

5th row and foll. alt. rows: K. the k. sts. and p. the p. sts. as they present themselves.

6th row: P.7, C. 4 B.P., C. 4 F., C. 4 F.P., p.7.

8th row: P.5, C. 4 B.P., p.2, k.4, p.2, C. 4 F.P., p.5

10th row: P.4, B.Cr., p.4, C. 4 F., p.4, F.Cr., p.4.

12th row: P.3, B.Cr., p.3, C. 4 B., C. 4 F., p.3, F.Cr., p.3.

14th row: P.2, B.Cr., p.2, C. 4 B.P., k.4, C. 4 F.P., p.2, FCr., p.2.

16th row: P.2, k.2, p.1, C. 4 B.P., p.2, C. 4 B., p.2, C. 4 F.P., p.1, k.2, p.2.

18th row: P.2, k.2, p.1, k.2, p.4, k.4, p.4., k.2, p.1, k.2, p.2.

20th row: P.2, k.2, p.1, C. 4 F.P., p.2, C. 4 B., p.2, C. 4 B.P., p.1, k.2, p.2.

22nd row: P.2, F.Cr., p.2, C. 4 F.P., k.4, C. 4 B.P., p.2, B.Cr., p.2.

24th row: P.3, F.Cr., p.3, C. 4 F.P., C. 4 B.P., p.3, B.Cr., p.3.

26th row: P.4, F.Cr., p.4, C. 4 F., p.4, B.Cr., p.4.

28th row: P.5, C. 4 F.P., p.2, k.4, p.2, C. 4 B.P., p.5.

30th row: P.7, C. 4 F.P., C. 4 F., C. 4 B.P., p.7.

32nd row: P.9, C. 4 F.P., C. 4 B.P., p.9.

These 32 rows form the pattern.

No. 71 **Wide Multi-cable Pattern** 49 sts.

A superb example of the Aran pattern craft. Tiny cables thread through bolder cables and are repeated as a side border.

C. 4 F., cable 4 front thus: slip next 2 sts. to front on cable needle, k.2, then k.2 from cable needle.

C. 4 B., cable 4 back thus: slip next 2 sts. to back on cable needle, k.2, then k.2 from cable needle.

Inc. loop p., pick up loop between sts. and p. in back of it.

1st row: (right side) (P.2, k.4) 4 times, p.1, (k.4, p.2) 4 times.

2nd, 4th, 6th and 8th rows: (K.2, p.4) 4 times, k.1, (p.4, k.2) 4 times.

3rd row: (P.2, C. 4 F., p.2, k.4) twice, p.1, (k.4, p.2, C. 4 B., p.2) twice.

5th row: As 1st row.

7th row: P.2, C. 4 F., p.2, k.4, p.2, C. 4 F., p.2, slip next 5 sts. to front on cable needle, k.4, then slip the p. st. back on to left hand needle and p. it, then k.4 from cable needle, p.2, C. 4 B., p.2, k.4, p.2, C. 4 B., p.2.

9th row: P.2, k.4, p.2, *inc. loop p., (k.4, p.2) twice, k.4, inc. loop p.*, p.1, rep. from * to *, p.2, k.4, p.2.

10th row: K.2, p.4, *k.3, p.4, (k.2, p.4) twice; rep. from * once more, k.3, p.4, k.2.

11th row: P.2, C. 4 F., p.3, inc. loop p., k.4, p. 2 tog., C. 4 F., p. 2 tog., k.4, inc. loop p., p.3, inc. loop p., k.4, p. 2 tog., C. 4 B., p. 2 tog., k.4, inc. loop p., p.3, C. 4 B., p.2.

12th row: K.2, p.4, k.4, *(p.4, k.1) twice, p.4*, k.5, rep. from * to *, k.4, p.4, k.2.

13th row: P.2, k.4, p.4, *inc. loop p., k.3, slip 1, k.1, p.s.s.o., k.4, k. 2 tog., k.3, inc. loop p.*, p.5, rep. from * to *, p.4, k.4, p.2.

14th row: K.2, p.4, k.5, p.12, k.7, p.12, k.5, p.4, k.2.

15th row: P.2, C. 4 F., p.5, inc. loop p., k.4, C. 4 F., k.4, inc. loop p., p.7, inc. loop p., k.4, C. 4 B., k.4, inc. loop p., p.5, C. 4 B., p.2.

16th row: K.2, p.4, k.6, p.12, k.9, p.12, k.6, p.4, k.2.

17th row: P.2, k.4, p.6, slip next 8 sts. to back on cable needle, k.4 from main needle, then slip the last 4 sts. from cable needle back on to left hand needle and k. them, then k.4 from cable needle (thus crossing the 8 sts.), p.9, slip next 8 sts. to front on cable needle, k.4 from main needle, slip the last 4 sts. from cable needle back on to left hand needle and k. them, then k.4 from cable needle, p.6, k.4, p.2.

18th, 20th, 22nd and 24th rows: Repeat 16th, 14th, 12th and 10th rows in that order.

19th row: P.2, C. 4 F., p.4, p. 2 tog., k.4, C. 4 F., k.4, p. 2 tog., p.5, p. 2 tog., k.4, C. 4 B., k.4, p. 2 tog., p.4, C. 4 B., p.2.

21st row: P.2, k.4, p.3, *p. 2 tog., (k.4, inc. loop p.) twice, k.4, p. 2 tog., p.3*; rep. from * to *, k.4, p.2.

23rd row: P.2, C. 4 F., p.2, p. 2 tog., k.4, inc. loop p., p.1, C. 4 F., p.1, inc. loop p., k.4, p. 2 tog., p.1, p. 2 tog., k.4, inc. loop p., p.1, C. 4 B., p.1, inc. loop p., k.4, p. 2 tog., p.2, C. 4 B., p.2.

25th row: P.2, k.4, p.1, p. 2 tog., * (k.4, p.2) twice, k.4*, p. 3 tog.; rep. from * to *, p. 2 tog., p.1, k.4, p.2.

26th row: As 2nd row.

27th row: As 7th row.

28th row: As 2nd row.

These 28 rows form the pattern.

78 *Wide multi-cable pattern*

6 The knitting patterns

Unlike the Guernsey or Jersey which is traditionally knitted in the round on five needles, the design of the Aran fishing shirt consists of a front, back and two sleeves. It, too, may have originally been worked by the circular method, since this was typical of most folk knitting. The straight cast off at the sleeve top indicates that these could have easily been worked from the armhole edge down towards the cuff, as in the Guernsey. However, at a later stage, perhaps with the advent of pairs of knitting needles and the greater complexity of the patterns, the design became the familiar garments with side and sleeve seams as shown in the earliest recorded pieces. Certainly, some of these show slight pattern differences in the back and front, say a cable crossed in the opposite direction.

For comfort and weatherproofing the traditional shirt is possibly second to none but since their inception knitted garments have undergone many changes, not least in design. The development of knitting styles started in the late Victorian era with the appeal for knitted articles by Florence Nightingale at the time of the Crimean war. At first the shaping of the knitted pieces was purely functional and for Aran knitting this meant developing from the fisherman's sweater, which only required straight shapes, into the sports sweater, with its variety of neckline, round, polo collar and V-neck. Much more recently knitting has become high fashion and the Aran knitting has come into its own. The intricate patterns are used to adorn everything, from luxury top fashion wear to the humble cushion cover.

The instructions for the articles in the following patterns have been given with the pattern panels first, with the method for construction in a wide range of sizes detailed subsequently. In this way the knitter can vary the panels used if desired, and the greatest combination of designs may be obtained.

PATTERN 1: TRADITIONAL FISHING SHIRT

This is a typical fishing shirt or sweater in the traditional Aran shape and patterns. It contains many forms of cable and other historic panels, such as ladder of life, wave of honey and Irish moss stitch.

Materials

950 [1000:1050:1100:1150] g 3 Suisses Gaelic Bainin yarn
A pair each 4 mm and 4½ mm (No. 8 and No. 7 UK: 5 and 6 USA) knitting needles
A cable needle
A set of four double-pointed knitting needles 4 mm (No. 8: 5)

Measurements

To fit 86 [91:97:102:107] cm (34 [36:38:40:42] in) chest; length, 62 [65:68:71:74] cm (24½ [25½:26½:28:29] in); sleeve seam, 43 [43:46:46:46] cm (17 [17:18:18:18] in)

Tension

19 sts. to 10 cm (4 in) over stocking stitch

Panel A   Aran Moss Stitch Even number of sts.

1st row: (K.1, p.1) to end.
2nd row: (K.1, p.1) to end.
3rd row: (P.1, k.1) to end.
4th row: (P.1, k.1) to end.
These 4 rows form the pattern.

Panel A   Aran Moss Stitch Odd number of sts.

1st row: K.1, (p.1, k.1) to end.
2nd row: P.1, (k.1, p.1) to end.
3rd row: As 2nd row.
4th row: As 1st row.
These 4 rows form the pattern.

Panel B   Gull Stitch 6 sts.

1st row: K.2, y.bk., slip 2 purlwise, k.2.
2nd row: P.2, y.fwd., slip 2 purlwise, p.2.
3rd row: Slip next 2 sts. to back on cable needle, k.1, then k.2 from cable needle, slip next st. to front on cable needle, k.2, then k.1 from cable needle.
4th row: P.
These 4 rows form the pattern.

Panel C   Ladder of Life

1st row: K.
2nd row: P.
3rd and 4th rows: P.
These 4 rows form the pattern.

Panel D   Marriage Lines 15 sts.

1st row: P.1, k.1, p.1, k.12.
2nd row: P.11, (k.1, p.1) twice.
3rd row: K.2, p.1, k.1, p.1, k.10.
4th row: P.9, k.1, p.1, k.1, p.3.
5th row: K.4, p.1, k.1, p.1, k.8.
6th row: P.7, k.1, p.1, k.1, p.5.
7th row: K.6, p.1, k.1, p.1, k.6.
8th row: P.5, k.1, p.1, k.1, p.7.
9th row: K.8, p.1, k.1, p.1, k.4.
10th row: P.3, k.1, p.1, k.1, p.9.

11th row: K.10, p.1, k.1, p.1, k.2.
12th row: (P.1, k.1) twice, p.11.
13th row: K.12, p.1, k.1, p.1.
14th row: (P.1, k.1) twice, p.11.
15th row: K.10, p.1, k.1, p.1, k.2.
16th row: P.3, k.1, p.1, k.1, p.9.
17th row: K.8, p.1, k.1, p.1, k.4.
18th row: P.5, k.1, p.1, k.1, p.7.
19th row: K.6, p.1, k.1, p.1, k.6.
20th row: P.7, k.1, p.1, k.1, p.5.
21st row: K.4, p.1, k.1, p.1, k.8.
22nd row: P.9, k.1, p.1, k.1, p.3.
23rd row: K.2, p.1, k.1, p.1, k.10.
24th row: P.11, (k.1, p.1) twice.
These 24 rows form the pattern.

Panel E   Wave of Honey 4 sts.
1st row: Slip next st. to back on cable needle, k.1, then k.1 from cable needle, slip next st. to front on cable needle, k.1, then k.1 from cable needle.
2nd row: P.
3rd row: Slip next st. to front on cable needle, k.1, then k.1 from cable needle, slip next st. to back on cable needle, k.1, then k.1 from cable needle.
4th row: P.
These 4 rows form the pattern.

Panel F   Aran Diamonds within Diamonds 18 sts.
1st row: K.1 t.b.l., p.5, k.1 t.b.l., p.1, (k.1 t.b.l.) twice, p.1, k.1 t.b.l., p.5, k.1 t.b.l.
2nd row: P.1 t.b.l., k.5, p.1 t.b.l., k.1, (p.1 t.b.l.) twice, k.1, p.1 t.b.l., k.5, p.1 t.b.l.
3rd row: K.1 t.b.l., p.4, (slip next st. to back on cable needle, k.1 t.b.l., p.1 from cable needle) twice, (slip next st. to front on cable needle, p.1, then k.1 t.b.l. from cable needle) twice, p.4, k.1 t.b.l.
4th row: P.1 t.b.l., k.4, p.1 t.b.l., k.1, p.1 t.b.l., k.2, p.1 t.b.l., k.1, p.1 t.b.l., k.4, p.1 t.b.l.
5th row: K.1 t.b.l., p.3, (slip next st. to back on cable needle, k.1 t.b.l., then p.1 from cable needle) twice, p.2, (slip next st. to front on cable needle, p.1, then k.1 t.b.l. from cable needle) twice, p.3, k.1 t.b.l.
6th row: P.1 t.b.l., k.3, p.1 t.b.l., k.1, p.1 t.b.l., k.4, p.1 t.b.l., k.1, p.1 t.b.l., k.3, p.1 t.b.l.
7th row: K.1 t.b.l., p.2, (slip next st. to back on cable needle, k.1 t.b.l., then p.1 from cable needle) twice but k.1 from cable needle on second repeat, p.4, (slip next st. to front on cable needle, k.1 t.b.l., then k.1 t.b.l. from cable needle) twice but p.1 from main needle on second repeat, p.2, k.1 t.b.l.
8th row: P.1 t.b.l., k.2, p.1 t.b.l., k.1, (p.1 t.b.l.) twice, k.4, (p.1 t.b.l.) twice, k.1, p.1 t.b.l., k.2, p.1 t.b.l.
9th row: K.1 t.b.l., p.1, (slip next st. to back on cable needle, k.1 t.b.l., p.1 from cable needle) twice, slip next st. to front

on cable needle, p.1, then k.1 t.b.l. from cable needle, p.2, slip next st. to back on cable needle, k.1 t.b.l., then p.1 from cable needle, (slip next st. to front on cable needle, p.1, then k.1 t.b.l. from cable needle) twice, p.1, k.1 t.b.l.

10th row: (P.1 t.b.l., k.1) twice, p.1 t.b.l., (k.2, p.1 t.b.l.) 3 times, (k.1, p.1 t.b.l.) twice.

11th row: K.1 t.b.l., (slip next st. to back on cable needle, k.1 t.b.l., then p.1 from cable needle) twice, p.2, slip next st. to front on cable needle, p.1, then k.1 t.b.l. from cable needle, slip next st. to back on cable needle, k.1 t.b.l., then p.1 from cable needle, p.2, (slip next st. to front on cable needle, p.1, k.1 t.b.l. from cable needle) twice, k.1 t.b.l.

12th row: (P.1 t.b.l.) twice, k.1, p.1 t.b.l., k.4, slip next st. to front on cable needle, p.1 t.b.l., p.1 from cable needle, k.4, p.1 t.b.l., k.1, (p.1 t.b.l.) twice.

13th row: K.1 t.b.l., (slip next st. to front on cable needle, p.1, then k.1 t.b.l. from cable needle) twice, p.2, slip next st. to back on cable needle, k.1 t.b.l., then p.1 from cable needle, slip next st. to front on cable needle, p.1, then k.1 t.b.l. from cable needle, p.2, (slip next st. to back on cable needle, k.1 t.b.l., then p.1 from cable needle) twice, k.1 t.b.l.

14th row: (P.1 t.b.l., k.1) twice, p.1 t.b.l., (k.2, p.1 t.b.l.) 3 times, (k.1, p.1 t.b.l.) twice.

15th row: K.1 t.b.l., p.1, (slip next st. to front on cable needle, p.1, then k.1 t.b.l. from cable needle) twice, slip next st. to back on cable needle, k.1 t.b.l., then p.1 from cable needle, p.2, slip next st. to front on cable needle, p.1, then k.1 t.b.l. from cable needle, (slip next st. to back on cable needle, k.1 t.b.l., then p.1 from cable needle) twice, p.1, k.1 t.b.l.

16th row: As 8th row.

17th row: K.1 t.b.l., p.2, (slip next st. to front on cable needle, p.1, then k.1 t.b.l. from cable needle) twice, p.4, (slip next st. to back on cable needle, k.1 t.b.l., then p.1 from cable needle) twice, p.2, k.1 t.b.l.

18th row: As 6th row.

19th row: K.1 t.b.l., p.3, (slip next st. to front on cable needle, p.1, then k.1 t.b.l. from cable needle) twice, p.2, (slip next st. to back on cable needle, k.1 t.b.l., then p.1 from cable needle) twice, p.3, k.1 t.b.l.

20th row: As 4th row.

21st row: K.1 t.b.l., p.4, (slip next st. to front on cable needle, p.1, then k.1 t.b.l. from cable needle) twice, (slip next st. to back on cable needle, k.1 t.b.l., then p.1 from cable needle) twice, p.4, k.1 t.b.l.

22nd row: P.1 t.b.l., k.5, p.1 t.b.l., k.1, slip next st. to front on cable needle, p.1 t.b.l., p.1 from cable needle, k.1, p.1 t.b.l., k.5, p.1 t.b.l.

Repeat 3rd to 22nd rows for pattern.

Back

With 4 mm (No. 8: 5) needles, cast on 98 [104:104:110: 116] sts.

1st row: (right side) K.1, *k.3, k.1 t.b.l., p.2; rep. from * to last st., k.1.

2nd row: K.1, *k.2, p.1 t.b.l., p.3; rep. from * to last st., k.1.

3rd row: K.1, *k.3, slip next st. to front on cable needle, p.1, then k.1 t.b.l. from cable needle, p.1; rep. from * to last st., k.1.

4th row: K.1, *k.1, p.1 t.b.l., k.1, p.3; rep. from * to last st., k.1.

5th row: K.1, *k.3, p.1, slip next st. to front on cable needle, p.1, then k.1 t.b.l. from cable needle; rep. from * to last st., k.1.

6th row: K.1, *p.1 t.b.l., k.2, p.3; rep. from * to last st., k.1.
Repeat the last 6 rows to form decorated welt, 3 [3:3:4:4] times more, ending last repeat after a 5th pattern row.

Inc. row: P.4 [7:6:3:6], *inc. 1 purlwise by picking up the loop between the sts. and p. in back of it, p.10 [10:7:8:8]; rep. from * to last 4 [7:7:3:6] sts., inc. 1 purlwise as before, p. to end. 108 [114:118:124:130] sts.
Change to 4½ mm (No. 7: 6) needles and work 2 rows garter stitch.

Now continue in pattern, placing the panels thus:

1st row: (right side) K.1, Panel A over 6 [6:8:10:12] sts., p.2, Panel B over 6 sts., p.2, Panel C over 3 [6:6:7:8] sts., p.2, Panel D over 15 sts., p.2, Panel E over 4 sts., p.2, Panel F over 18 sts., p.2, Panel E over 4 sts., p.2, Panel D over 15 sts., p.2, Panel C over 3 [6:6:7:8] sts., p.2, Panel B over 6 sts., p.2, Panel A over 6 [6:8:10:12] sts., k.1.

2nd row: K.1, Panel A over 6 [6:8:10:12] sts., k.2, Panel B over 6 sts., k.2, Panel C over 3 [6:6:7:8] sts., k.2, Panel D over 15 sts., k.2, Panel E over 4 sts., k.2, Panel F over 18 sts., k.2, Panel E over 4 sts., k.2, Panel D over 15 sts., k.2, Panel C over 3 [6:6:7:8] sts., k.2, Panel B over 6 sts., k.2, Panel A over 6 [6:8:10:12] sts., k.1.
Continue in pattern with panels as now set, having p.2 between panels on right side rows and k.2 between panels on wrong side rows, until work measures 39 [41:43:46:48] cm (15½ [16¼:17:18:19¼] in), ending after a wrong side row. Mark both ends of last row to indicate beginning of armhole.
Continue in pattern as before marked row until work measures 58 [61:64:67:69] cm (23 [24:25½:26½:27½] in) from cast on edge, ending after a wrong side row.

Shape Shoulder Edges

Cast off 37 [39:41:43:45] sts. at beginning of next 2 rows.
Leave remaining 34 [36:36:38:40] sts. on spare needle.

Front

Work exactly as given for back.

Sleeves

With 4 mm (No. 8: 5) needles, cast on 48 [48:52:52:56] sts.
Work 8 cm (3¼ in) k.2, p.2 rib.
Inc. row: (wrong side) P.6 [6:5:7:6] sts., *inc. 1 purlwise by picking up the loop between the sts. and p. in back of it, p. 5

79 OPPOSITE *Traditional fishing shirt, pattern 1*

80 *Detail of panels on fishing shirt, pattern 1*

[4:6:3:4]; rep. from * to last 7 [6:5:6:6] sts., inc. 1 purlwise as before between sts., p. to end. 56 [58:60:66:68] sts.

Change to 4½ mm (No. 7:6) needles and work in pattern, placing panels thus:

1st row: Panel A over 3 [4:5:8:9] sts., p.2, Panel B over 6 sts., p.2, Panel E over 4 sts., p.2, Panel F over 18 sts., p.2, Panel E over 4 sts., p.2, Panel B over 6 sts., p.2, Panel A over 3 [4:5:8:9] sts.

Continue in pattern with panels as now set, having p.2 between panels on right side rows and k.2 between panels on wrong side rows, inc. 1 st. at both ends of 5th row following and every following 5th [5th:5th:6th:6th] row, working all inc. sts. in Panel A until there are 82 [88:92:96:100] sts.

Continue in pattern until sleeve measures 43 [43:46:46:46] cm (17 [17:18:18:18] in), ending after a wrong side row.

Cast off 31 [34:36:38:40] sts. at beginning of next 2 rows.

Continue on remaining 20 sts. in Panel F with k.1 at both ends of every row until sleeve extension fits across cast off sts. at shoulder.

Leave remaining sts. on spare needle.

Collar

Press pieces lightly, avoiding ribbed sections.

Join side edges of sleeve extensions to cast off sts. at shoulders on front and back.

With right side of work facing, using set of double pointed needles 4 mm (No. 8: 5), k.34 [36:36:38:40] sts. from back neck, 20 sts. from sleeve extension, 34 [36:36:38:40] sts. from

front neck and 20 sts. from second sleeve extension. 108 [112:112:112:116:120] sts.
Work 10 cm (4 in) in rounds of k.2, p.2 rib.
Cast off sts. in rib.

To make up
Join cast off 31 [34:36:38:40] sts. at top of sleeve to armhole edge above markers. Join side and sleeve seams. Press seams.

PATTERN 2: TRADITIONAL FISHING SHIRT
Again in the traditional shape, this sweater uses a different a different combination of the authentic Aran patterns.

Materials
950 [1000:1050:1100:1150] g 3 Suisses Gaelic Bainin yarn
A pair each 4 mm and 4½ mm (No. 8 and No. 7 UK: 5 and 6 USA) knitting needles
A cable needle
A set of four double-pointed needles 4 mm (No. 8: 5)

Measurements
To fit 86 [91:97:102:107] cm (34 [36:38:40:42] in) chest; length, 62 [65:68:71:74] cm (24½ [25½:26½:28:29] in); sleeve seam, 43 [43:46:48:51] cm (17 [17:18:19:20] in)

Tension
19 sts. to 10 cm (4 in) over stocking stitch.

Special Abbreviations
C. 4 F., cable 4 front thus: slip next 2 sts. to front on cable needle, k.2, then k.2 from cable needle.
C. 4 B., cable 4 back thus: slip next 2 sts. to back on cable needle, k.2, then k.2 from cable needle.
C. 2 B., cable 2 back thus: slip next st. to back on cable needle, k.1 t.b.l., then p.1 from cable needle.
C. 2 F., cable 2 front thus: slip next st. to front on cable needle, p.1, then k.1 t.b.l. from cable needle.
Cr. 2 F.K., cross 2 front knit thus: slip next st. to front on cable needle k.1, then k.1 t.b.l. from cable needle.
Cr. 2 B.K., cross 2 back knit thus: slip next st. to back on cable needle, k.1 t.b.l., then k.1 from cable needle.
Tw. 2, twist 2 thus: k. second st. on left hand needle, then k. first st. and slip both loops off together.
F.Cr., front cross thus: slip next 2 sts. to front on cable needle, p.1, then k.2 from cable needle.
B.Cr., back cross thus: slip next st. to back on cable needle, k.2, then p.1 from cable needle.

Panel A   Moss Stitch Uneven number of stitches
Pattern row: K.1, (p.1, k.1) to end.
Repeat this 1 row for pattern.

Panel A   Moss Stitch Even number of stitches
1st row: (K.1, p.1) to end.
2nd row: (P.1, k.1) to end.
These 2 rows form the pattern.

Panel B   Jacob's Ladder 7 sts.
1st and 3rd rows: P.1, k.5, p.1.
2nd and 4th rows: K.1, p.5, k.1.
5th row: (right side) P.7.
6th row: As 2nd and 4th rows.
These 6 rows form the pattern.

Panel C   Zigzag and Irish Moss Stitch 7 sts.
1st row: (right side) F.Cr., p.4.
2nd row and foll. alt. rows: K. the k. sts. and p. the p. sts. as they present themselves.
3rd row: K.1, F.Cr., p.3.
5th row: P.1, k.1, F.Cr., p.2.
7th row: K.1, p.1, k.1, F.Cr., p.1.
9th row: (P.1, k.1) twice, F.Cr.
11th row: (K.1, p.1) twice, B.Cr.
13th row: P.1, k.1, p.1, B.Cr., p.1.
15th row: K.1, p.1, B.Cr., p.2.
17th row: P.1, B.Cr., p.3.
19th row: B.Cr., p.4.
20th row: As 2nd row.
Repeat 1st to 20th rows, reversing zigzag when this panel occurs at the other end of the row.

Panel D   Tree of Life 9 sts.
1st row: K.1 t.b.l., p.2, k.3 t.b.l., p.2, k.1 t.b.l.
2nd row: K.3, p.3 t.b.l., k.3.
3rd row: P.2, slip next st. to back on cable needle, k.1 t.b.l., then p.1 from cable needle, k.1 t.b.l., slip next st. to front on cable needle, p.1, then k.1 from cable needle, p.2.
4th row: K.2, p.1 t.b.l., k.1, p.1 t.b.l., k.1, p.1 t.b.l., k.2.
5th row: P.1, slip next st. to back on cable needle, k.1 t.b.l., then p.1 from cable needle, p.1, k.1 t.b.l., p.1, slip next st. to front on cable needle, p.1, k.1 t.b.l. from cable needle, p.1.
6th row: K.1, p.1 t.b.l., k.2, p.1 t.b.l., k.2, p.1 t.b.l., k.1.
7th row: Slip next st. to back on cable needle, k.1 t.b.l., then p.1 from cable needle, p.1, k.3 t.b.l., p.1, slip next st. to front on cable needle, p.1, k.1 t.b.l. from cable needle.
8th row: K.3, p.3 t.b.l., k.3.
9th row: P.2, slip next st. to back on cable needle, k.1 t.b.l., p.1 from cable needle, k.1 t.b.l., slip next st. to front on cable needle, p.1, then k.1 from cable needle, p.2.
10th row: K.2, p.1 t.b.l., k.1, p.1 t.b.l., k.1, p.1 t.b.l., k.2.
Repeat 5th to 10th rows for pattern.

Panel E   Bobble Strip Pattern 8 sts.
1st to 4th rows: Beginning k. row, in st.-st.
5th row: K.3, make bobble thus: k. into front, back, front, back, front of next st., making 5 sts. out of 1 st., k. next st., turn and p.5, turn and k.5, turn and p.5, turn and slip 2nd, 3rd, 4th and 5th sts. over 1st st., k. in back of bobble st., k.3.
6th to 10th rows: Beginning p. row, in st.-st.
Repeat 5th to 10th rows for pattern.

Panel F 4 sts.

1st row: Slip next st. to front on cable needle, k.1, then k.1 from cable needle, slip next st. to back on cable needle, k.1, then k.1 from cable needle.

2nd and 4th rows: P.4.

3rd row: Slip next st. to back on cable needle, k.1, then k.1 from cable needle, slip next st. to front on cable needle, k.1, then k.1 from cable needle.

These 4 rows form the pattern.

Panel G   Centre Panel 36 sts.

1st row: K.4, p.1, (k.1 t.b.l., p.1) 6 times, k.2 t.b.l., (p.1, k.1 t.b.l.) 6 times, p.1, k.4.

2nd row: P.4, k.1, (p.1 t.b.l., k.1) 6 times, p.2 t.b.l., (k.1, p.1 t.b.l.) 6 times, k.1, p.4.

3rd row: C. 4 F., (p.1, k.1 t.b.l.) 4 times, (C. 2 B.) 3 times, (C. 2 F.) 3 times, (k.1 t.b.l., p.1) 4 times, C. 4 B.

4th row: P.4, k.1, (p.1 t.b.l., k.1) 3 times, p.2 t.b.l., (k.1, p.1 t.b.l.) twice, k.2, (p.1 t.b.l., k.1) twice, p.2 t.b.l., (k.1, p.1 t.b.l.) 3 times, k.1, p.4.

5th row: K.4, p.1, (k.1 t.b.l., p.1) 3 times, (C. 2 B.) 3 times, Tw. 2, (C. 2 F.) 3 times, (p.1, k.1 t.b.l.) 3 times, p.1, k.4.

6th row: P.4, k.1, (p.1 t.b.l., k.1) 6 times, p.2, (k.1, p.1 t.b.l.) 6 times, k.1, p.4.

7th row: C. 4 F., (p.1, k.1 t.b.l.) 3 times, (C. 2 B.) 3 times, p.1, Tw.2, p.1, (C. 2 F.) 3 times, (k.1 t.b.l., p.1) 3 times, C. 4 B.

8th row: P.4, (k.1, p.1 t.b.l.) 3 times, (p.1 t.b.l., k.1) 3 times, k.1, p.2, k.1, (k.1, p.1 t.b.l.) 3 times, (p.1 t.b.l., k.1) 3 times, p.4.

9th row: K.4, (p.1, k.1 t.b.l.) twice, p.1, (C. 2 B.) 3 times, p.2, Tw.2, p.2, (C. 2 F.) 3 times, (p.1, k.1 t.b.l.) twice, p.1, k.4.

10th row: P.4, (k.1, p.1 t.b.l.) 5 times, k.3, p.2, k.3, (p.1 t.b.l., k.1) 5 times, p.4.

11th row: C. 4 F., (p.1, k.1 t.b.l.) twice, (C. 2 B.) 3 times, p.3, Tw.2, p.3, (C. 2 F.) 3 times, (k.1 t.b.l., p.1) twice, C. 4 B.

12th row: P.4, (k.1, p.1 t.b.l.) twice, (p.1 t.b.l., k.1) 3 times, k.3, p.2, k.3, (k.1, p.1 t.b.l.) 3 times, (p.1 t.b.l., k.1) twice, p.4.

13th row: K.4, p.1, k.1 t.b.l., p.1, (C. 2 B.) 3 times, p.4, Tw.2, p.4, (C. 2 F.) 3 times, p.1, k.1 t.b.l., p.1, k.4.

14th row: P.4, (k.1, p.1 t.b.l.) 4 times, k.5, p.2, k.5, (p.1 t.b.l., k.1) 4 times, p.4.

15th row: C. 4 F., p.1, k.1 t.b.l., (C. 2 B.) 3 times, p.5, Tw.2, p.5, (C. 2 F.) 3 times, k.1 t.b.l., p.1, C. 4 B.

16th row: P.4, k.1, p.2 t.b.l., (k.1, p.1 t.b.l.) twice, k.6, p.2, k.6, (p.1 t.b.l., k.1) twice, p.2 t.b.l., k.1, p.4.

17th row: K.4, p.1, k.1 t.b.l., (C. 2 F.) 3 times, p.5, Tw.2, p.5, (C. 2 B.) 3 times, k.1 t.b.l., p.1, k.4.

18th row: P.4, k.1, (p.1 t.b.l., k.1) 4 times, k.4, p.2, k.5, (p.1

81 *Traditional fishing shirt, pattern 2*

t.b.l., k.1) 4 times, p.4.

19th row: C. 4 F., p.1, k.1 t.b.l., p.1, C 2 F.K., (C. 2 F.) twice, p.4, Tw.2, p.4, (C. 2 B.) twice, C. 2 B.K., p.1, k.1 t.b.l., p.1, C. 4 B.

20th row: P.4, (k.1, p.1 t.b.l.) twice, (p.1 t.b.l., k.1) 3 times, k.3, p.2, k.3, (k.1, p.1 t.b.l.) 3 times, (p.1 t.b.l., k.1) twice, p.4.

21st row: K.4, (p.1, k.1 t.b.l.) twice, (C. 2 F.) 3 times, p.3, Tw.2, p.3, (C. 2 B.) 3 times, (k.1 t.b.l., p.1) twice, k.4.

22nd row: P.4, (k.1, p.1 t.b.l.) 5 times, k.3, p.2, k.3, (p.1 t.b.l., k.1) 5 times, p.4.

23rd row: C. 4 F., (p.1, k.1 t.b.l.) twice, p.1, C. 2 F.K., (C. 2 F.) twice, p.2, Tw.2, p.2, (C. 2 B.) twice, C. 2 B.K., (p.1, k.1 t.b.l.) twice, p.1, C. 4 B.

24th row: P.4, k.1, (p.1 t.b.l., k.1) twice, p.2 t.b.l., (k.1, p.1 t.b.l.) twice, k.2, p.2, k.2, (p.1 t.b.l., k.1) twice, p.2 t.b.l., (k.1, p.1 t.b.l.) twice, k.1, p.4.

25th row: K.4, p.1, (k.1 t.b.l., p.1) twice, k.1 t.b.l., (C. 2 F.)

3 times, p.1, Tw.2, p.1, (C. 2 B.) 3 times, (k.1 t.b.l., p.1) 3 times, k.4.

26th row: P.4, (k.1, p.1 t.b.l.) 6 times, k.1, p.2, k.1, (p.1 t.b.l., k.1) 6 times, p.4.

27th row: C. 4 F., p.1, (k.1 t.b.l., p.1) 3 times, C. 2 F.K., (C. 2 F.) twice, Tw.2, (C. 2 B.) twice, C. 2 B.K., (p.1, k.1 t.b.l.) 3 times, p.1, C. 4 B.

28th row: P.4, (k.1, p.1 t.b.l.) 4 times, (p.1 t.b.l., k.1) twice, p.1 t.b.l., p.2., p.1 t.b.l., (k.1, p.1 t.b.l.) twice, (p.1 t.b.l., k.1) 4 times, p.4.

29th row: K.4, (p.1, k.1 t.b.l.) 4 times, (C. 2 F.) 3 times, (C. 2 B.) 3 times, (k.1 t.b.l., p.1) 4 times, k.4.

Repeat 2nd to 29th rows for pattern.

Back

With 4 mm (No. 8: 5) needles, cast on 124 [128:132:136:140] sts.

Work in Panel F, placing sts. thus:

1st row: (right side) P.3 [2:1:3:2], *work 1st row of Panel F over next 4 sts., p.2; rep. from * ending last rep. p.3[2:1:3:2], instead of p.2.

2nd row: K.3 [2:1:3:2], *work 2nd row of Panel F over next 4 sts., k.2; rep. from * ending last rep. k.3 [2:1:3:2].

Work remaining 2 rows of Panel F on following 2 rows, then repeat the 4 rows pattern as set until 48 rows have been completed.

Change to 4½ mm (No. 7: 6) needles and continue in panels of pattern, placing the panels thus:

1st row: (right side) Panel A over 1 [3:5:7:9] sts., Panel B over 7 sts., p.1, k.1 t.b.l., Panel C over 7 sts., k.1 t.b.l., p.2, Panel D over 9 sts., Panel E over 8 sts., p.2, Panel F over 4 sts., p.1, Panel G over 36 sts., p.1, Panel F over 4 sts., p.2, Panel E over 8 sts., Panel D over 9 sts., p.2, k.1 t.b.l., Panel C over 7 sts., k.1 t.b.l., p.1, Panel B over 7 sts., Panel A over 1 [3:5:7:9] sts.

2nd row: Panel A over 1 [3:5:7:9] sts., Panel B over 7 sts., k.1, p.1, Panel C over 7 sts., p.1, k.2, Panel D over 9 sts., Panel E over 8 sts., k.2, Panel F over 4 sts., k.1, Panel G over 36 sts., k.1, Panel F over 4 sts., k.2, Panel E over 8 sts., Panel D over 9 sts., k.2, p.1, Panel C over 7 sts., p.1, k.1, Panel B over 7 sts., Panel A over 1 [3:5:7:9] sts.

Continue in pattern with panels as now set, until work measures 39 [41:43:46:48] cm (15½ [16¼:17:18:19¼] in), ending after a wrong side row. Mark both ends of last row to indicate beginning of armhole.

Continue in pattern as before marked row until work measures 58 [61:64:67:69] cm (23 [24:25½:26½:27½] in) from cast on edge, ending after a wrong side row.

Shape Shoulder Edges

Cast off 39 [41:43:45:47] sts. at beginning of next 2 rows.
Leave remaining 46 sts. on spare needle.

Front
Work exactly as given for back.

Sleeves
With 4 mm (No. 8: 5) needles, cast on 48 sts.
Work 8 cm (3¼ in) pattern as back welt, placing sts. thus:
1st row: (right side) P.1, *Panel F over next 4 sts., p.2; rep. from * ending last rep. p.1.
End cuff after a right side row.
Inc. row: (K.1, panel F over 4 sts., k.1) twice, (k.1, inc. in next st.) 12 times, (k.1, Panel F over 4 sts., k.1) twice. 60 sts.
Change to 4½ mm (No. 7:6) needles and continue in pattern placing the panels thus:
1st row: (right side) Panel A over 5 sts., p.2, Panel F over 4 sts., p.1, Panel G over 36 sts., p.1, Panel F over 4 sts., p.2, Panel A over 5 sts.
2nd row: Panel A over 5 sts., k.2, Panel F over 4 sts., k.1, Panel G over 36 sts., k.1, Panel F over 4 sts., k.2, Panel A over 5 sts.
Continue in pattern with panels as now set, inc. 1 st. at both ends of next row following and every following 5th row until there are 84 [88:92:96:100] sts., working inc. sts. in Panel A.
Continue in pattern until sleeve measures 43 [43:46:48:51] cm (17 [17:18:19:20] in), ending after a wrong side row.
Cast off 28 [30:32:34:36] sts. at beginning of next 2 rows.
Continue in pattern on remaining 28 sts. until sleeve extension fits across cast off sts. at shoulder.
Leave the remaining sts. on spare needle.

Collar
Press pieces lightly, avoiding welts and cuffs.
Join side edges of sleeve extensions to cast off sts. at shoulders on front and back.
With right side of work facing, using set of double-pointed needles 4 mm (No. 8:5), k. 46 sts. from back next, k. 28 sts. from left sleeve extension, dec. 2 sts. evenly across, k. 46 sts.

82 *Detail of panels on fishing shirt, pattern 2*

from front neck, k. 28 sts. from right sleeve extension, dec. 2 sts. evenly across. 144 sts.

Work 10 cm (4 in) in rounds of Panel F, placing pattern thus: *(Panel F over 4 sts., p.2) 7 times, Panel F over 4 sts.* across 46 sts., **(p.2, Panel F over 4 sts.) 4 times, p.2** across 26 sts., repeat from * to * across next 46 sts., then from ** to ** across next 26 sts.

Cast off sts.

To Make Up

Join cast off 28 [30:32:34:36] sts. at top of sleeve to armhole edge above markers. Join side and sleeve seams.

Press seams.

83 *Detail showing sleeve extension joined to shoulder, pattern 2*

PATTERN 3: TRADITIONAL FISHING SHIRT

The panels for this sweater have been taken from a picture of what may be the earliest garment of its kind to be recorded (see page 17). Although the patterns may not appear as complex as others they are of historic interest since they were worked in the days when patterns would have been passed down from mother to daughter, before instructions were written in the present style.

One size only is given for this sweater to cover the number of stitches required to produce all the panels in the original garment. A variation in the size could be made by omitting the outer 15 sts. of Panel B and replacing them with more or less stitches in a simple flat pattern, say reverse stocking stitch, to accommodate the larger or smaller finished size.

Materials

1250g 3 Suisses Gaelic Bainin yarn
A pair each 4 mm and 4½ mm (No. 8 and No. 7 UK: 5 and 6 USA) knitting needles
A cable needle
A set of four double-pointed needles 4 mm (No. 8: 5)

Measurements

To fit 112 cm (44 in) chest; length, 68 cm (26½ in); sleeve seam, 48 cm (19 in).

Tension

19 sts. to 10 cm (4 in) in stocking stitch.

Special Abbreviations

L.Tw., left twist thus: p. t.b.l. in second st. on left hand needle, k. first st. and slip both loops off together.

R.Tw., right twist thus: k. second st. on left hand needle, p. first st. and slip both loops off together.

C. 4 F. t.b.l., cable 4 front t.b.l. thus: slip next 2 sts. to front on cable needle, k.2 t.b.l., then k.2 t.b.l. from cable needle.

Panel A   Rib and Twist Cable 8 sts. plus 3

1st row: (right side) *K.3, p.1, k.1 t.b.l., p.1, k.1 t.b.l., p.1; rep. from * to last 3 sts., k.3.

2nd row: P.3, *k.1, p.1 t.b.l., k.1, p.1 t.b.l., k.1, p.3; rep. from * to end.

3rd to 6th rows: Rep. 1st and 2nd rows twice.

7th row: *K.3, p.1, slip next 2 sts. to front on cable needle, k.1 t.b.l., (p.1, k.1 t.b.l.) both from cable needle, p.1; rep. from * to last 3 sts., k.3.

8th row: As 2nd row.

These 8 rows form the pattern.

Panel B   Moss Stitch Diamond on Knit Background

15 sts.

1st row: (right side) K.

2nd row: P.7, k.1, p.7.

3rd row: K.6, (p.1, k.1) twice, k.5.

4th row: P.5, (k.1, p.1) 3 times, p.4.

5th row: K.4, (p.1, k.1) 4 times, k.3.

6th row: P.3, (k.1, p.1) 5 times, p.2.

7th row: K.2, (p.1, k.1) 6 times, k.1.

8th row: P.1, (k.1, p.1) 7 times.

9th row: P.1, (k.1, p.1) 7 times.

10th row: As 8th row.

11th to 16th rows: As 7th to 2nd rows in backward rotation.

These 16 rows form the pattern.

Panel C   Twist Stitch Zigzag 12 sts.

1st row: (right side) P.1, (L.Tw.) twice, p.7.

2nd row: K.6, (L.Tw.) twice, k.2.

3rd row: P.3, (L.Tw.) twice, p.5.

4th row: K.4, (L.Tw.) twice, k.4.

5th row: P.5, (L.Tw.) twice, p.3.

6th row: K.2, (L.Tw.) twice, k.6.

7th row: P.7, (L.Tw.) twice, p.1.

8th row: K. the k. sts. and p. the p. sts. as they present themselves.

9th row: P.7, (R.Tw.) twice, p.1.

10th row: K.2, (R.Tw.) twice, k.6.

11th row: P.5, (R.Tw.) twice, p.3.

12th row: K.4, (R.Tw.) twice, k.4.
13th row: P.3, (R.Tw.) twice, p.5.
14th row: K.6, (R.Tw.) twice, k.2.
15th row: P.1, (R.Tw.) twice, p.7.
16th row: As 8th row.
These 16 rows form the pattern.

Panel D Aran Diamond and Twist Stitch Rib 13 sts.

1st row: (right side) P.5, slip next 2 sts. to front on cable needle, k.1 t.b.l., then (p.1, k.1 t.b.l.) both from cable needle, p.5.
2nd row: K.5, p.3, k.5.
3rd row: P.4, slip next st. to back on cable needle, k.1 t.b.l., then p.1 from cable needle—called B.Cr., k.1 t.b.l., slip next st. to front on cable needle, p.1, then k.1 t.b.l. from cable needle—called F.Cr., p.4.
4th row and foll. alt. rows: K. the k. sts. and p. the p. sts. as they present themselves.
5th row: P.3, B.Cr. *knitting* both sts. t.b.l., p.1, k.1 t.b.l., p.1, F.Cr. knitting both sts. t.b.l., p.3.
7th row: P.2, B.Cr., (k.1 t.b.l., p.1) twice, k.1 t.b.l., F.Cr., p.2.
9th row: P.2, F.Cr., (k.1 t.b.l., p.1) twice, k.1 t.b.l., B.Cr., p.2.
11th row: P.3, F.Cr., p.1, k.1 t.b.l., p.1, B.Cr., p.3.
13th row: P.4, F.Cr., p.1, B.Cr., p.4.
14th row: K.5, p.1, k.1, p.1, k.5.
These 14 rows form the pattern.

Panel E Six-stitch Cable Front 10 sts.

1st row: (right side) P.2, k.6, p.2.
2nd row: K.2, p.6, k.2.
3rd row: P.2, slip next 3 sts. to front on cable needle, k.3, then k.3 from cable needle, p.2.
4th row: As 2nd row.
5th to 8th rows: Repeat 1st and 2nd rows twice.
These 8 rows form the pattern.

Panel F Trellis with Moss Stitch 28 sts.

1st row: (right side) P.5, C. 4 F. t.b.l., p.10, C. 4 F. t.b.l., p.5.
2nd row and foll. alt. rows: K. the k. sts. and p. the p. sts. as they present themselves.
3rd row: P.4, slip next st. to back on cable needle, k.2 t.b.l., then p.1 from cable needle—called B.Cr., slip next 2 sts. to front on cable needle, k.1, then k.2 t.b.l. from cable needle—called F.Cr., p.8, B.Cr., F.Cr., p.4.
5th row: P.3, (B.Cr., k.1, p.1, F.Cr.), p.6, repeat bracketed portion once more, p.3.
7th row: P.2, B.Cr., (k.1, p.1) twice, F.Cr., p.4, B.Cr., (k.1, p.1) twice, F.Cr., p.2.
9th row: P.1, B.Cr., (k.1, p.1) 3 times, F.Cr., p.2, B.Cr., (k.1, p.1) 3 times, F.Cr., p.1.
11th row: *B.Cr., (k.1, p.1) 4 times, F.Cr.; rep. from * once more.

13th row: K.2 t.b.l., (k.1, p.1) 5 times, C. 4 F. t.b.l., (k.1, p.1) 5 times, k.2 t.b.l.

15th row: *Slip next 2 sts. to front on cable needle, p.1, then k.2 t.b.l. from cable needle—called F.Cr.P., (k.1, p.1) 4 times, B.Cr.; rep. from * once more.

17th row: P.1, F.Cr.P., (k.1, p.1) 3 times, B.Cr., p.2, F.Cr.P., (k.1, p.1) 3 times, B.Cr., p.1.

19th row: P.2, F.Cr.P., (k.1, p.1) twice, B.Cr., p.4, F.Cr.P., (k.1, p.1) twice, B.Cr., p.2.

21st row: P.3, F.Cr.P., k.1, p.1, B.Cr., p.6, F.Cr.P., k.1, p.1, B.Cr., p.3.

23rd row: P.4, F.Cr.P., B.Cr., p.8, F.Cr.P., B.Cr., p.4.

24th row: As 2nd row.

These 24 rows form the pattern.

Panel G   Twist Rib Cable 11 sts.

1st row: (right side) P.2, (k.1 t.b.l., p.1) 4 times, p.1.

2nd row: K.2, (p.1, k.1) 4 times, k.1.

3rd to 6th rows: As 1st and 2nd rows.

7th row: P.2, slip next 4 sts. to front on cable needle, (k.1 t.b.l., p.1) twice, then (k.1 t.b.l., p.1) twice from cable needle, p.1.

8th row: As 2nd row.

9th to 12th rows: Rep. 1st and 2nd rows twice.

These 12 rows form the pattern.

Panel H   Single Lattice Pattern Multiple of 8 sts.

1st row: (right side) P.3, slip next st. to back on cable needle, k.1, then k.1 from cable needle—called B.Cr., *p.6, B.Cr.; rep. from * ending p.3.

2nd row and foll. alt. rows: K. the k. sts. and p. the p. sts. as they present themselves.

3rd row: P.2, *B.Cr.P. (as B.Cr. but p.1 from cable needle), F.Cr.P. (as F.Cr. but p.1, then k.1 from cable needle), p.4; rep. from * ending B.Cr.P., F.Cr.P., p.2.

5th row: P.1, *B.Cr.P., p.2, F.Cr.P., p.2; rep. from * ending B.Cr.P., p.2, F.Cr.P., p.1.

7th row: *B.Cr.P., p.4, F.Cr.P.; rep. from * to end.

9th row: K.1, *p.6, F.Cr.; rep. from * ending p.6, k.1.

11th row: *F.Cr.P., p.4, B.Cr.P.; rep. from * to end.

13th row: P.1, *F.Cr.P., p.2, B.Cr.P., p.2; rep. from * ending F.Cr.P., p.2, B.Cr.P., p.1.

15th row: P.2, *F.Cr.P., B.Cr.P., p.4; rep. from * ending F.Cr.P., B.Cr.P., p.2.

16th row: As 2nd row.

Back

With 4 mm (No. 8: 5) needles, cast on 131 sts.

Work 48 rows in Panel A.

Change to 4½ mm (No. 7: 6) needles.

K. 6 rows, dec. 3 sts. across last row. 128 sts.

Now continue in pattern placing sts. thus:

1st row: Panel B over 15 sts., Panel C over 12 sts., Panel D

84 *Traditional fishing shirt, pattern 3*

over 13 sts., Panel E over 10 sts., Panel F over 28 sts., Panel
E over 10 sts., Panel D over 13 sts., Panel C over 12 sts.,
Panel B over 15 sts.

Continue in pattern with panels as now set until the 8th row
of the fourth Panel B moss stitch diamond has been worked.
Mark both ends of last row to indicate beginning of
armholes. Continue in pattern as before marked row until 7½
diamond patterns have been worked, ending after a wrong
side row.

Shape Shoulder Edges

Cast off 45 sts. at beginning of next 2 rows.
Leave remaining 38 sts. on spare needle.

Front

Work exactly as given for back.

Sleeves

With 4½ mm (No. 7: 6) needles, cast on 74 sts.

1st row: K.3, *p.2, k.4; rep. from * ending last rep., k.3.

2nd row: P.3, *k.2, p.4; rep. from * ending last rep., p.3.

Rep. last 2 rows until rib measures 10 cm (4 in), ending after a 2nd row and inc. 1 st. at both ends of last row. 76 sts.

Do not change needles but continue in pattern, placing the panels thus:

1st row: (right side) P.2, Panel D over 13 sts., Panel G over 11 sts., Panel H over 24 sts., Panel G over 11 sts., Panel D over 13 sts., p.2.

2nd row: K.2, Panel D over 13 sts., Panel G over 11 sts., Panel H over 24 sts., Panel G over 11 sts., Panel D over 13 sts., k.2.

Continue in pattern with panels as now set, inc. 1 st. at both ends of next row following and every following 4th row to 104 sts.

Work the inc. sts. in Panel C when possible, then when this panel has 12 sts., work remaining sts. in reverse st.-st. (p. side is right side).

Now continue in pattern, inc. 1 st. at both ends of every following 8th row to 110 sts.

Continue in pattern until 10½ repeats of Panel G have been worked. Inc. 1 st. at both ends of next 6 rows. 122 sts.

Cast off 49 sts. at beginning of next 2 rows.

Continue in moss stitch on remaining 24 sts. until sleeve extension fits across cast off sts. at shoulder.

Leave remaining sts. on spare needle.

Collar

Press pieces lightly, avoiding welts and cuffs.

Join side edges of sleeve extensions to cast off sts. at shoulders on front and back.

With right side of work facing, using set of double-pointed needles 4 mm (No. 8: 5), k. 38 sts. from back neck, 24 sts. from sleeve extension, 38 sts. from front neck and 24 sts. from other sleeve extension. 124 sts.

Work 10 cm (4 in) in rounds of k.2, p.2 rib.

Cast off sts. in rib.

To Make Up

Join cast off 49 sts. at top of sleeve to armhole edge above markers. Join side and sleeve seams.

Press seams.

PATTERN 4: FAMILY SWEATER. ROUND NECK

These casual sweaters (patterns 4–6) are modern in design and there are instructions for three different necklines for each size. The panels, although traditional, are quite simple and the shaping is worked in moss stitch.

Materials

450 [500:550:600:700:800:900:950:1050] g Sirdar Bainin Aran yarn
A pair each 3¼ mm and 4½ mm (No. 10 and No. 7 UK: 3 and 6 USA) knitting needles
A cable needle

Measurements

To fit 66 [71:76:81:86:91:97:102:107] cm (26 [28:30:32:34:36:38:40:42] in) chest/bust; length, 47 [51:53:55:58:61:64:67:68] cm (18½ [20:20½:21½:22½:24:25½:26½:26¾] in); sleeve seam, 30 [34:38:40:43:43:44:46:48] cm (12 [13½:15:16:17:17:17½:18:19] in)

85 *Family sweaters with Valentine cable centre panel, patterns 4 and 5*

Tension

19 sts. to 10 cm (4 in) over stocking stitch

Special Abbreviations

C. 4 F., cable 4 sts. front thus: slip next 2 sts. to front on cable needle, k.2, then k.2 from cable needle.

B.Cr., back cross thus: slip next st. to back on cable needle, k.2, then p.1 from cable needle.

F.Cr., front cross thus: slip next 2 sts. to front on cable needle, p.1, then k.2 from cable needle.

Panel A Double Moss Stitch Even number of sts.

1st and 2nd rows: (K.1, p.1) to end.

3rd and 4th rows: (P.1, k.1) to end.

Panel A Double Moss Stitch Uneven number of sts.

1st row: (K.1, p.1) to last st., k.1.

2nd row: (P.1, k.1) to last st., p.1.

3rd row: As 2nd row.

4th row: As 1st row.

These 4 rows form the pattern.

Panel B Trinity Stitch 4 sts. plus 2

1st row: (right side) P.

2nd row: K.1, *p. 3 tog., k.1-p.1-k.1 all in next st.; rep. from * to last st., k.1.

3rd row: P.

4th row: K.1, *k.1-p.1-k.1 all in next st., p. 3 tog.; rep. from * to last st., k.1.

Panel C Cable Pattern 13 sts.

1st row: K.1, *p.1, C. 4 F.; rep. from * once more, p.1, k.1.

2nd row: P.1, k.1, p.4, k.1, p.4, k.1, p.1.

3rd row: K.1, p.1, k.4, p.1, k.4, p.1, k.1.

4th row: As 2nd row.

5th to 8th rows: Rep. 3rd and 4th rows twice.

These 8 rows form the pattern.

Panel D Valentine Cable Pattern 18 sts.

1st row: (right side) P.7, C. 4 F., p.7.

2nd row: K.7, p.4, k.7.

3rd row: P.6, B.Cr., F.Cr., p.6.

4th row: K.6, p.2, k.2, p.2, k.6.

5th row: P.5, B.Cr., p.2, F.Cr., p.5.

6th row: K.5, p.2, k.4, p.2, k.5.

7th row: P.4, B.Cr., p.4, F.Cr., p.4.

8th row: K.4, p.2, k.6, p.2, k.4.

9th row: P.3, (B.Cr.) twice, (F.Cr.) twice, p.3.

10th row: K.3, (p.2, k.1, p.2, k.2) twice, ending k.3.

11th row: P.2, (B.Cr.) twice, p.2, (F.Cr.) twice, p.2.

12th row: K.2, p.2, k.1, p.2, k.4, p.2, k.1, p.2, k.2.

13th row: P.2, k.1, slip next st. to front on cable needle, p.1, then k.1 from cable needle, F.Cr., p.2, B.Cr., slip next st. to back on cable needle, k.1, then p.1 from cable needle, k.1, p.2.

14th row: K.2, p.1, k.1, p.1, k.1, p.2, k.2, p.2, k.1, p.1, k.1, p.1, k.2.

15th row: P.2, k.1, p.1, cross 1 front as 13th row, F.Cr., B.Cr., cross 1 back as 13th row, p.1, k.1, p.2.

16th row: K.2, p.1, k.2, p.1, k.1, p.4, k.1, p.1, k.2, p.1, k.2.

17th row: P.2, cross 1 front as 13th row, cross 1 back as 13th row, p.1, C. 4 F., p.1, cross 1 front as 13th row, cross 1 back as 13th row, p.2.

18th row: K.3, slip next st. to back on cable needle, k.1, then k.1 from cable needle, k.2, p.4, k.2, slip next st. to front on cable needle, k.1, then k.1 from cable needle, k.3.

Repeat 3rd to 18th rows for pattern.

Back

With 3¼ mm (No. 10: 3) needles, cast on 70 [74:80:84:90:96:100:106:112] sts.

Work 4 [4:4:5:6:8:8:8:8] cm (1½ [1½:1½:2:2½:3¼:3¼:3¼:3¼] in) k.1, p.1 rib.

Inc. row: (wrong side) P.8 [6:9:7:10:9:7:10:13] sts., (p. twice in next st., p.3) 14 [16:16:18:18:20:22:22:22] times, ending last repeat, p. 9 [7:10:8:11:10:8:11:14]. 84 [90:96:102:108:116:122:128:134] sts.

Change to 4½ mm (No. 7: 6) needles and continue in pattern, placing panels thus:

1st row: Panel A over 6 [9:12:11:14:18:17:20:23] sts., Panel B over 14 [14:14:18:18:18:22:22:22] sts., Panel C over 13 sts.,

86 *Round neck collar version, pattern 4*

Panel D over 18 sts., Panel C over 13 sts., Panel B over 14 [14:14:18:18:18:22:22:22] sts., Panel A over 6 [9:12:11:14:18:17:20:23] sts.

Continue in pattern with panels as now set until work measures 33 [35:35:36:38:39:41:43:43] cm (13 [13¾:13¾:14¼:15:15½:16:17:17] in) ending after a wrong side row.

Shape Armholes

Cast off 4 sts. at beginning of next 2 rows. **
Dec. 1 st. at both ends of every row to 64 [68:72:76:80:84:88:92:96] sts. ***
Continue straight in pattern until armholes measure 14 [16:18:19:20:22:23:24:25] cm (5½ [6¼:7:7½:8:8½:9:9½:10] in) ending after a wrong side row.

Shape Shoulders

Cast off 6 [6:6:6:7:8:8:9:9] sts. at beginning of next 4 rows; 7 [8:9:9:9:8:10:9:10] sts. at beginning of next 2 rows.
Leave remaining 26 [28:30:34:34:36:36:38:40] sts. on spare needle.

Front

Work as back to ***.
Continue straight in pattern until armholes measure 12 [13:14:15:16:17:18:18:18] cm (4¾ [5:5½:6:6½:6¾:7:7:7] in) ending after a wrong side row.

Shape Neck

Next row: Pattern 37 [39:42:44:47:49:52:55:58] sts., slip last 10 [10:12:12:14:14:16:18:20] sts. worked on to spare needle, pattern to end. Continue in pattern on last set of sts. only.
Dec. 1 st. at neck edge on every row until 19 [20:21:21:23:24:26:27:28] sts. remain. Continue straight until armhole matches back to shoulder, ending at side edge.

Shape Shoulder

Cast off 6 [6:6:6:7:8:8:9:9] sts. at beginning of next row and following alternate row. Work 1 row. Cast off remaining sts. With wrong side of work facing, join yarn to remaining sts. and work this side to match first side, reversing shapings.

Sleeves

With 3¼ mm (No. 10: 3) needles, cast on 32 [34:36:36:38:40:44:44:46] sts.
Work 5 [5:5:8:8:8:8:10:10] cm (2 [2:2:3¼:3¼:3¼:3¼:4:4] in) k.1, p.1 rib.
Inc. row: P. 2 [3:6:2:5:4:8:6:7] sts., (p. twice in next st., p.1) 14 [14:12:16:14:16:14:16:16] times, p. 2 [3:6:2:5:4:8:6:7]. 46 [48:48:52:54:56:58:60:62] sts.
Change to 4½ mm (No. 7: 6) needles and continue in pattern placing panels thus:
1st row: Panel A over 1 [2:2:4:5:6:7:8:9] sts., Panel C over 13 sts., Panel D over 18 sts., Panel C over 13 sts., Panel A over 1 [2:2:4:5:6:7:8:9] sts.

Continue in pattern with panels as now set and keeping inc. sts. in Panel A, inc. 1 st. at both ends of 7th [13th:11th:9th:11th:11th:5th:9th:9th] row then every following 10th [10th:10th:12th:12th:11th:11th:8th:8th:8th] row to 54 [56:58:64:68:70:76:80:82] sts.

Continue straight until sleeve measures 30 [34:38:40:43:43:44:46:48] cm (12 [13½:15:16:17:17:17½:18:19] in) ending after a wrong side row.

Shape Top

Cast off 4 sts. at beginning of next 2 rows.

Dec. 1 st. at both ends of next 6 [7:8:9:10:12:13:14:15] rows, then every following alternate row to 10 [12:12:14:14:14:16:18:18] sts., ending after a wrong side row.

Cast off remaining sts.

Collar

Join right shoulder seam.

With right side of work facing, using 3¼ mm (No. 10: 3) needles, pick up and k. 72 [76:80:86:90:94:100:108:114] sts. evenly round neck edge, including sts. on spare needles. Work 5 [5:5:5:5:5:5:6:6] cm (2 [2:2:2:2:2:2:2½:2½] in) k.1, p.1 rib. Cast off sts. loosely in rib.

To Make Up

Join left shoulder seam and collar seam. Join side and sleeve seams. Sew in sleeves.

Fold collar in half to wrong side and slip stitch.

A simple classic neckband may be made by working half the given collar depth before casting off the sts. Do not fold this neckband to wrong side, simply close the neckband seam.

Press seams lightly, omitting ribbed sections.

PATTERN 5: FAMILY SWEATER. V-NECK

The details of materials, measurements and tension etc. for this garment are given at the beginning of the previous pattern, the round neck sweater, on page 83.

Back and Sleeves

Work exactly as given for back and sleeves of round neck sweater, pattern 4, page 83.

Front

Work as back of round neck sweater, pattern 4, to **.

Divide for V-neck

Next row: K. 2 tog., pattern 34 [37:40:43:46:50:53:56:59] sts., k. 2 tog., turn. Complete this side first.

Dec. 1 st. at armhole edge on next 5 [6:7:8:9:11:12:13:14] rows, *at the same time*, dec. 1 st. at neck edge on every right side row. Keeping armhole edge straight, dec. at neck edge only on every following 3rd row until 19 [20:21:21:23:24:26:27:28] sts. remain. Continue straight until armhole matches back to shoulder, ending after a wrong side row.

87 *Detail of panels on family sweaters, patterns 4, 5 and 6*

88 *V-neck collar for sportswear, pattern 5*

Shape Shoulder

Cast off 6 [6:6:6:7:8:8:9:9] sts. at beginning of next row and following alternate row. Work 1 row. Cast off remaining sts. With right side of work facing, join yarn to remaining sts., k. 2 tog., pattern to last 2 sts., k. 2 tog. Complete this side to match first side, reversing shapings.

Collar

Join right shoulder seam.
With right side of work facing, using $3\frac{1}{4}$ mm (No. 10: 3) needles, k. 26 [28:30:34:34:36:36:38:40] sts. from back neck, pick up and k. 35 [37:39:41:45:47:49:51:53] sts. down left front neck, pick up and k. 1 st. at centre of 'V' and mark this st., pick up and k. 36 [38:40:42:46:48:50:52:54] sts. up right front neck. 98 [102:110:118:126:132:136:142:148] sts.
Keeping the marked st. as k. on right side rows and p. on wrong side rows, work 6 rows k.1, p.1 rib, dec. 1 st. at both sides of marked st. on every row.
Cast off sts. in rib, dec. as before.

To Make Up

Join left shoulder and neckband seam. Join side and sleeve seams. Sew in sleeves.

Press seams lightly avoiding ribbed sections.

PATTERN 6: FAMILY SWEATER. POLO NECK

The main pieces of this sweater are similar to the round neck sweater, pattern 4, page 83. Details of materials, measurements, tension etc. will be found at the beginning of pattern 4 instructions. A further 50 g yarn will be required for each size.

Back, Front and Sleeves

Work exactly as given for back, front and sleeves of round neck sweater, pattern 4, page 83.

Collar

Join right shoulder seam.

With right side of work facing, using $3\frac{1}{4}$ mm (No. 10: 3) needles, pick up and k. 72 [76:80:86:90:94:100:108:114] sts. evenly round neck edge, including sts. on spare needles. Work 4 [4:4:4:5:5:5:5:5] cm ($1\frac{1}{2}$ [$1\frac{1}{2}$:$1\frac{1}{2}$:$1\frac{1}{2}$:2:2:2:2:2] in) k.1, p.1 rib. Change to $4\frac{1}{2}$ mm (No. 7: 6) needles and work a further 5 [5:5:5:6:6:7:7:8] cm (2 [2:2:2:$2\frac{1}{2}$:$2\frac{1}{2}$:$2\frac{3}{4}$:$2\frac{3}{4}$:$3\frac{1}{4}$] in) rib. Cast off sts. loosely in rib.

89 *The family sweater with polo collar, pattern 6*

To Make Up

Join left shoulder seam and collar, reversing seam at fold line.
Join side and sleeve seams. Sew in sleeves.
Press seams lightly, avoiding ribbed sections.
Fold polo collar to right side.

PATTERN 7: V-NECK, RAGLAN-SHAPED CARDIGAN

Symbolic Aran diamond and Irish moss stitch decorated with bobbles are used for the main panels on this raglan-shaped cardigan. It has a wide range of sizes and is suitable for men, women and children

Materials

320 [360:400:480:520:560:640:680:760] g Wendy Aran machine washable yarn
A pair each $3\frac{1}{4}$ mm and $4\frac{1}{2}$ mm (No. 10 and No. 7 UK: 3 and 6 USA) knitting needles
A cable needle
5 [5:6:6:7:8:8:9:9] buttons

Measurements

To fit 66 [71:76:81:86:91:97:102:107] cm (26 [28:30:32:34:36:38:40:42] in) chest/bust; length, 42 [46:49:57:60:61:63:65:66] cm ($16\frac{1}{2}$ [18:$19\frac{1}{2}$:$22\frac{1}{2}$:$23\frac{1}{2}$:24:25:$25\frac{1}{2}$:26] in); sleeve seam, 30 [34:38:43:43:43:44:46:46] cm (12 [$13\frac{1}{2}$:15:17:17:17:$17\frac{1}{2}$:18:18] in).

Tension

19 sts. to 10 cm (4 in) over stocking stitch.

Special Abbreviations

D.M. stitch, double moss stitch thus:
1st and 2nd rows: (K.1, p.1) over given number of sts.
3rd and 4th rows: (P.1, k.1) over given number of sts.
C. 2 F., cable 2 front thus: slip next st. to front on cable needle, k.1, then k.1 from cable needle.
C. 2 B., cable 2 back thus: slip next st. to back on cable needle, k.1, then k.1 from cable needle.
M.B., make bobble thus: (k.1, p.1, k.1, p.1, k.1, p.1, k.1) all in next st., slip 2nd, 3rd, 4th, 5th, 6th and 7th sts. on right hand needle over first st.—bobble made.
F.Cr., front cross thus: slip next 2 sts. to front on cable needle, p.1, then k.2 from cable needle.
B.Cr., back cross thus: slip next st. to back on cable needle, k.2, then p.1 from cable needle.

Panel A   Aran Diamond, Irish Moss and Bobble Pattern 15 sts.

1st row: (right side) P.5, k.2, M.B., k.2, p.5.
2nd row: K.5, p.5, k.5.
3rd row: P.5, M.B., k.3, M.B., p.5.
4th row: As 2nd row.

90 *Raglan shaping is used for the popular V-neck cardigan, pattern 7*

5th row: As 1st row.
6th row: As 2nd row.
7th row: P.4, B.Cr., p.1, F.Cr., p.4.
8th row: K.4, p.2, k.1, p.1, k.1, p.2, k.4.
9th row: P.3, B.Cr., k.1, p.1, k.1, F.Cr., p.3.
10th row: K.3, p.3, k.1, p.1, k.1, p.3, k.3.
11th row: P.2, B.Cr., (p.1, k.1) twice, p.1, F.Cr., p.2.
12th row: K.2, p.2, (k.1, p.1) 3 times, k.1, p.2, k.2.
13th row: P.2, k.3, (p.1, k.1) twice, p.1, k.3, p.2.
14th row: As 12th row.
15th row: P.2, F.Cr., (p.1, k.1) twice, p.1, B.Cr., p.2.
16th row: As 10th row.
17th row: P.3, F.Cr., k.1, p.1, k.1, B.Cr., p.3.
18th row: As 8th row.

19th row: P.4, F.Cr., p.1, B.Cr., p.4.
20th row: As 2nd row.
These 20 rows form the pattern.

Back

With 3¼ mm (No. 10: 3) needles, cast on 70 [74:80:84:90:96:100:106:112] sts.
Work 4 [4:5:5:5:6:6:6:8] cm (1½ [1½:2:2:2½:2½:2½:2½:3¼] in) in k.1, p.1 rib.
Inc. row: (wrong side) P. 8 [6:10:7:10:9:7:10:13] sts., (p. twice in next st., p.3) 14 [16:16:18:18:20:22:22:22] times, ending last repeat p. 9 [7:9:8:11:10:8:11:14], instead of p.3.
84 [90:96:102:108:116:122:128:134] sts.
Change to 4½ mm (No. 7: 6) needles and continue in pattern, placing panels thus:
1st row: K. 1 [0:1:0:1:1:0:1:0] sts., D.M. stitch over next 6 [8:8:12:12:12:16:18:20] sts., p.2, C. 2 F., C. 2 B., Panel A over next 15 sts., (C. 2 F., C. 2 B., p.2) 1 [1:2:2:2:2:2:3:3] times, D.M. stitch over next 16 [20:12:12:16:24:24:12:16] sts., (p.2, C. 2 F., C. 2 B.) 1 [1:2:2:2:2:2:3:3] times, Panel A over next 15 sts., C. 2 F., C. 2 B., p.2, D.M. stitch to end.
2nd row: D.M. stitch over 7 [8:9:12:13:13:16:19:20] sts., k.2, p.4, Panel A over next 15 sts., (p.4, k.2) 1 [1:2:2:2:2:2:3:3] times, D.M. stitch over next 16 [20:12:12:16:24:24:12:16] sts., (k.2, p.4) 1 [1:2:2:2:2:2:3:3] times, Panel A over next 15 sts., p.4, k.2, D.M. stitch to end.
Continue in pattern with subsequent rows of Panel A until back measures 25 [28:30:36:38:38:38:38:38] cm (10 [11:12:14½:15:15:15:15:15] in), ending after a wrong side row.

Shape Raglan

Cast off 4 sts. at beginning of next 2 rows.
3rd row: K.2, k. 2 tog., t.b.l., pattern to last 4 sts., k. 2 tog., k.2.
4th row: K.2, p.1, pattern to last 3 sts., p.1, k.2.
8th size only
Next row: K.3, pattern to last 3 sts., k.3.
Next row: As 4th row.
All sizes
Repeat 3rd and 4th rows until 30 [32:38:42:44:50:46:48:50] sts. remain, ending after a 4th row.
3rd, 4th, 5th and 6th sizes only
Next row: As 3rd row.
Next row: K.2, p. 2 tog., pattern to last 4 sts., p. 2 tog. t.b.l., k.2.
6th size only
Repeat last 2 rows once more.
All sizes
Cast off remaining 30 [32:34:38:40:42:46:48:50] sts.

Left Front

With 3¼ mm (No. 10: 3) needles, cast on 33 [35:38:40:43:46:48:51:54] sts.

Work 4 [4:5:5:5:6:6:8:8] cm (1½ [1½:2:2:2:2½:2½:3¼:3¼] in) k.1, p.1 rib, beginning alternate rows p.1 on 1st, 2nd, 5th and 8th sizes.

Inc. row: (wrong side) P.4 [3:4:3:5:5:3:5:6], (inc. in next st., p.3) 7 [8:8:9:9:10:11:11:11] times, ending last repeat p. 4 [3:5:4:5:4:4:5:7] instead of p.3. 40 [43:46:49:52:56:59:62:65] sts.

Change to 4½ mm (No. 7: 6) needles and continue in pattern placing panels thus:

1st row: K. 1 [0:1:0:1:1:0:1:0] sts., D.M. stitch over next 6 [8:8:12:12:12:16:18:20] sts., p.2, C. 2 F., C. 2 B., Panel A over next 15 sts., (C. 2 F., C. 2 B., p.2) 1 [1:2:2:2:2:2:3:3] times, D.M. stitch to end.

Continue in pattern with panels as now set until front matches back to beginning of raglan shaping, ending after a wrong side row.

Shape Raglan and Begin Neck Shaping

1st row: Cast off 4 sts., pattern to last 2 sts., k. 2 tog.
Next row: Pattern to end.
3rd row: K.2, k. 2 tog. t.b.l., pattern to last 2 sts., k. 2 tog.
4th row: Pattern to last 3 sts., p.1, k.2.
8th size only
Next row: K.3, pattern to last 2 sts., k. 2 tog.
Next row: Pattern to last 3 sts., p.1, k.2.
All sizes
Dec. 1 st. at both ends as 3rd row on following 5 [5:5:8:8:8:9:8:10] right side rows, then at front edge on every following 4th row, *at the same time*, dec. at raglan edge on every right side row until 2 sts. remain. Dec. at raglan edge only until 1 st. remains. Fasten off.

Right Front

Work as left front, reversing shapings.
Place panels thus:
1st row: D.M. stitch over 6 [8:4:4:6:8:10:4:6], (p.2, C. 2 F., C. 2 B.) 1 [1:2:2:2:2:2:3:3] times, Panel A over next 15 sts., C. 2 F., C. 2 B., p.2, D.M. stitch to end.

Sleeves

With 3¼ mm (No. 10: 3) needles, cast on 32 [34:36:36:38:40:44:44:46] sts. Work 6 [6:6:8:8:8:9:9:9] cm (2½ [2½:2½:3¼:3¼:3¼:3½:3½:3½] in) k.1, p.1 rib, inc. 1 st. at end of last row. 33 [35:37:37:39:41:45:45:47] sts.

Inc. row: (wrong side) P. 5 [4:7:3:4:5:9:7:8], (p. twice in next st., p.1) 12 [14:12:16:16:16:14:16:16] times, ending last repeat p. 5 [4:7:3:4:5:9:7:8]. 45 [49:49:53:55:57:59:61:63] sts.

Change to 4½ mm (No. 7: 6) needles and continue in pattern placing panels thus:

1st row: D.M. stitch over 3 [5:5:7:2:3:4:5:6] sts., (p.2, C. 2 F., C. 2 B.) 2 [2:2:2:3:3:3:3:3] times, Panel A over next 15 sts., (C. 2 F., C. 2 B., p.2) 2 [2:2:2:3:3:3:3:3] times, D.M. stitch to end.

Continue in pattern with panels as now set, inc. 1 st. at both ends of 7th [13th:11th:9th:11th:11th:5th:9th:9th] row and every following 10th [13th:12th:13th:11th:11th:9th:8th:8th] row to 55 [57:59:65:69:71:77:81:83] sts., working inc. sts. in D.M. stitch.

Continue straight until sleeve measures 30 [34:38:43:43:44:46:46] cm (12 [13½:15:17:17:17:17½:18:18] in) ending after a wrong side row.

Shape Raglan

Cast off 4 sts. at beginning of next 2 rows.

3rd row: K.2, k.2 tog. t.b.l., pattern to last 4 sts., k. 2 tog., k.2.

4th row: K.2, p.1, pattern to last 3 sts., p.1, k.2.

5th row: K.3, pattern to last 3 sts., k.3.

6th row: As 4th row.

2nd and 3rd sizes only

Repeat 5th and 6th rows once more.

All Sizes

Repeat 3rd and 4th rows until 9 sts. remain, ending after a 4th row.

Next row: K.2, k.2 tog. t.b.l., p.1, k.2 tog., k.2.

Next row: K.2, p.3, k.2.

Cast off remaining sts. loosely.

Neckband

Join raglan seams.

For women's and girls' cardigans, mark left front with pins to represent buttons, the top one to be level with beginning of neck shaping and the lowest one to be 4 rows from cast on edge. Space remaining pins for required number of buttons equally between.

For men's and boys' cardigans, mark the right front in the same way.

With 3¼ mm (No. 10: 3) needles, cast on 11 sts.

1st row: K.2, *p.1, k.1; rep. from * to last st., k.1.

2nd row: K.1, *p.1, k.1; rep. from * to end.

Repeat last 2 rows until band, slightly stretched, fits front edge, round neck and sleeve tops, to beginning of neck shaping on second side. Now continue rib, working buttonholes to correspond with pinned positions thus:

1st row: Rib 4, cast off 3 sts., rib to end.

2nd row: Rib 4, cast on 3 sts., rib to end.

When all buttonholes have been worked, work 4 rows rib. Cast off sts. in rib.

To Make Up

Join side and sleeve seams.

Sew on neckband, having buttonholes on right front for women's and girls' cardigan and left front for men's and boys' cardigan.

Press seams lightly, avoiding ribbed sections.

Sew buttons to left front for women's and girls' cardigan, to right front for men's and boys' cardigan.

91 *Detail of panels on V-neck cardigan, pattern 7*

PATTERN 8: CABLE-PATTERNED WAISTCOATS

Bold cable panels are used for this waistcoat which can be made in nine different sizes to suit all the family.

Materials

300 [350:400:450:500:550:600:650:700] g Lister/Lee Aran quality yarn
A pair each 3¼ mm and 4½ mm (No. 10 and No. 7 UK: 3 and 6 USA) knitting needles
A cable needle
5 [5:6:6:7:7:7:8:8] buttons

Measurements

To fit 66 [71:76:81:86:91:97:102:107] cm (26 [28:30:32:34:36:38:40:42] in); length, 40 [44:47:54:56:58:59:60:61] cm (15¾ [17½:18½:21:22:22½:23:23½:24] in)

Tension

19 sts. to 10 cm (4 in) over stocking stitch

Special Abbreviations

Tw.2, twist 2 thus:
1st row: K. second st. on left hand needle, then k. first st. and slip both loops off together.

2nd row: P. second st. on left hand needle, then p. first st. and slip both loops off together.

F.Cr., front cross thus: slip next 2 sts. to front on cable needle, p.1, then k.2 from cable needle.

B.Cr., back cross thus: slip next st. to back on cable needle, k.2, then p.1 from cable needle.

Panel A   Ring Cable Pattern 8 sts.

1st row: K.

2nd row: P.

3rd row: Slip next 2 sts. to front on cable needle, p.2, then k.2 from cable needle, slip next 2 sts. to back on cable needle, k.2, then p.2 from cable needle.·

4th and 6th rows: K.2, p.4, k.2.

5th row: P.2, k.4, p.2.

7th row: Slip next 2 sts. to back on cable needle, k.2, then k.2 from cable needle, slip next 2 sts. to front on cable needle, k.2, then k.2 from cable needle.

8th row: P.

These 8 rows form the pattern.

Panel B   Braided Cable Pattern 16 sts.

1st row: K.2, p.4, k.4, p.4, k.2.

2nd row and foll. alt. rows: K. the k. sts. and p. the p. sts. as they present themselves.

3rd row: K.2, p.4, slip next 2 sts. to back on cable needle, k.2, then k.2 from cable needle, p.4, k.2.

5th row: F.Cr., p.2, B.Cr., F.Cr., p.2, B.Cr.

7th row: P.1, F.Cr., B.Cr., p.2, F.Cr., B.Cr., p.1.

9th row: P.2, C. 4 B. as 3rd row, p.4, C. 4 B. as 3rd row, p.2.

11th row: P.2, k.4, p.4, k.4, p.2.

13th row: As 9th row.

15th row: P.1, B.Cr., F.Cr., p.2, B.Cr., F.Cr., p.1.

17th row: B.Cr., p.2, F.Cr., B.Cr., p.2, F.Cr.

19th row: As 3rd row.

20th row: As 2nd row.

These 20 rows form the pattern.

Back

With $3\frac{1}{4}$ mm (No. 10: 3) needles, cast on 70 [74:80:84:90:96:100:106:112] sts.

Work 4 [4:4:5:5:5:5:5:5] cm ($1\frac{1}{2}$ [$1\frac{1}{2}$:$1\frac{1}{2}$:2:2:2:2:2:2] in) k.1, p.1 rib.

Inc. row: (wrong side) P. 8 [6:10:7:10:9:7:10:13], (p. twice in next st., p.3) 14 [16:16:18:18:20:22:22:22] times, ending last repeat p. 9 [7:9:8:11:10:8:11:14], instead of p.3. 84 [90:96:102:108:116:122:128:134] sts.

Change to $4\frac{1}{2}$ mm (No. 7: 6) needles and continue in pattern placing panels thus:

1st row: (right side) P. 0 [3:6:9:12:16:19:22:25], *p.2, Panel A over next 8 sts., p.2, Tw.2, p.2, Panel B over next 16 sts., p.2, Tw.2*, repeat from * to * once more, p.2, Panel A over next 8 sts., p. to end.

2nd row: K. 0 [3:6:9:12:16:19:22:25], *k.2, Panel A over next

8 sts., k.2, Tw.2, k.2, Panel B over next 16 sts., k.2, Tw.2*, repeat from * to * once more, k.2, Panel A over next 8 sts., k. to end.

Continue in pattern with panels as now set until work measures 25 [28:30:36:38:38:38:38:38] cm (10 [11:12:14:15:15:15:15:15] in) ending after a wrong side row.

Shape Armholes
Cast off 4 sts. at beginning of next 2 rows.
Keeping pattern correct, dec. 1 st. at both ends of every row until 72 [78:84:88:92:92:96:96:100] sts. remain. Dec. 1 st. at both ends of next row and following alternate rows to 64 [68:72:76:80:84:88:92:96] sts.
Continue straight, working edge sts. in reverse st.-st. (p. side is right side) where a complete pattern is not possible, until armholes measure 15 [16:17:18:18:20:21:22:23] cm (4¾ [5¼:6¼:7:7½:8:8¼:8¾:9] in) ending after a wrong side row.

Shape Shoulders
Cast off 6 [6:6:6:7:8:8:9:9] sts. at beginning of next 4 rows; 7 [8:9:9:9:8:10:9:10] sts. at beginning of next 2 rows.
Cast off remaining 26 [28:30:34:34:36:36:38:40] sts. loosely.

Left Front
With 3¼ mm (No. 10: 3) needles, cast on 31 [33:36:38:41:44:46:49:52] sts.
Work rib welt as back, beginning alternate rows p.1 on 1st, 2nd, 5th and 8th sizes.
Inc. row: (wrong side) P. 3 [2:3:2:4:4:2:4:5], (p. twice in next st., p.3) 7 [8:8:9:9:10:11:11:11] times, ending last repeat, p. 3 [2:4:3:4:3:3:4:6] instead of p.3. 38 [41:44:47:50:54:57:60:63] sts.
Change to 4½ mm (No. 7: 6) needles and continue in pattern, placing panels thus:
1st row: P. 0 [3:6:9:12:16:19:22:25], repeat from * to * on back, p.2.
Continue in pattern with panels as now set until front is 10 rows less than back to beginning of armhole shaping, ending at side edge.

Shape Front Slope
Dec. 1 st. at end of next row and at same edge on every following 3rd row until 34 [37:40:43:46:50:53:56:59] sts. remain, thus ending at side edge after a dec. row.

Shape Armhole and continue front edge shaping
Cast off 4 sts., pattern to end.
Next row: Pattern to end.
Next row: K. 2 tog., pattern to last 2 sts., k. 2 tog.
Continue dec. at neck edge on every following 3rd row, *at the same time,* dec. at armhole edge on following 1 [1:1:2:3:7:8:11:12] rows, then on following 4 [5:6:6:6:4:4:2:2] alternate rows.
Continue dec. at front edge until 19 [20:21:21:23:24:26:27:28] sts. remain.

93 *Cable patterned waistcoat*

Continue in pattern until armhole matches back to shoulder, ending at armhole edge.

Shape Shoulder

Cast off 6 [6:6:6:7:8:8:9:9] sts. at beginning of next row and following alternate row. Work 1 row. Cast off remaining 7 [8:9:9:9:8:10:9:10] sts.

Right Front

Work as left front, reversing shapings and working Panel B, then Panel A when repeating from * to * on back.

Armbands

Join shoulder seams.
With right side of work facing, using 3¼ mm (No. 10: 3)

needles, pick up and k. 78 [84:88:92:98:102:106:110:114] sts. evenly round armhole edge.

Work 6 rows k.1, p.1 rib, dec. 1 st. at both ends of right side rows.

Cast off remaining sts. in rib, dec. as before.

Front Bands

Mark left front for women's and girls' waistcoat, right front for men's or boys' waistcoat, with pins to represent buttons. The top one to be level with beginning of neck shaping, the lowest to be 3 rows from cast on edge. Space the remaining pins for required number of buttons equally between.

With 3¼ mm (No. 10: 3) needles, cast on 11 sts.

1st row: k.2, *p.1, k.1; rep. from * to last st., k.1.

2nd row: K.1, *p.1, k.1; rep. from * to end.

Repeat last 2 rows until band, slightly stretched, fits one front edge, round neck to beginning of neck shaping on second front. Continue in rib, working buttonholes to correspond with pinned positions thus:

1st row: Rib 4, cast off 3 sts., rib to end.

2nd row: Rib 4, cast on 3 sts., rib to end.

When all buttonholes have been worked, work 2 rows more. Cast off rib.

To Make Up

Join side seams and armbands.

Sew on front bands, having buttonholes on right front for women's and girls' waistcoat, on left front for men's and boys'.

Press seams, avoiding ribbed sections.

Sew buttons to left front band for women's and girls' waistcoat, to right front band for men's and boys' waistcoat.

94 *Detail of panels on waistcoat, pattern 8*

95 *This waistcoat is in children's and adult sizes, pattern 8*

PATTERN 9: EASY KNIT JACKETS

A jacket that would suit all the family, coming in nine sizes. The back is in stocking stitch and the front and sleeves have just one Aran panel, making it ideal for a beginner to knit.

Materials

600 [650:750:850:950:1050:1100:1150:1250] g Lister/Lee Aran quality yarn
A pair each 4 mm and 4½ mm (No. 8 and No. 7 UK: 5 and 6 USA) knitting needles
A cable needle

Measurements

To fit 66 [71:76:81:86:91:97:102:107] cm (26 [28:30:32:34:36:38:40:42] in) chest/bust; length, 44 [49:54:60:61:62:64:66:67] cm (17½ [19¼:21:23½:24:24½:25½:26:26½] in); sleeve seam, 30 [33:36:38:42:43:44:46] cm (11¾ [13:14:15:16½:17:17:17½:18] in)

Tension

19 sts. to 10 cm (4 in) over stocking stitch

Special Abbreviation

Tw.2, twist 2 thus: (right side) K. second st. on left hand needle, then k. first st. and slip both loops off together.

Panel A   Fan Rib and Bobble 19 sts.

1st row: (wrong side) K.2, p.2, (k.1, p.1 t.b.l.) 5 times, k.1, p.2, k.2.

2nd row: P.7, k.2, (p.1, k.1, p.1, k.1, p.1) all in next st., turn and k.5, turn and p.5, slip 2nd, 3rd, 4th and 5th sts. over 1st st.—bobble made, k.2, p.7.

3rd row: K.7, p.2, p.1 t.b.l., p.2, k.7.

4th row: P.6, slip next st. to back on cable needle, k.2, then p.1 from cable needle—called B.Cr., k.1 t.b.l., slip next 2 sts. to front on cable needle, p.1, then k.2 from cable needle—called F.Cr., p.6.

5th row: K.6, p.2, k.1, p.1 t.b.l., k.1, p.2, k.6.

6th row: P.5, B.Cr. *but* k.1 t.b.l. from cable needle, p.1, k.1 t.b.l., p.1, F.Cr. *but* k.1 t.b.l. from main needle, p.5.

7th row: K.5, p.2, (p.1 t.b.l., k.1) twice, p.1 t.b.l., p.2, k.5.

8th row: P.4, B.Cr., (k.1 t.b.l., p.1) twice, k.1 t.b.l., F.Cr., p.4.

9th row: K.4, p.2, (k.1, p.1 t.b.l.) 3 times, k.1, p.2, k.4.

10th row: P.3, B.Cr. as 6th row, (p.1, k.1 t.b.l.) 3 times, p.1, F.Cr. as 6th row, p.3.

11th row: K.3, p.2, (p.1 t.b.l., k.1) 4 times, p.1 t.b.l., p.2, k.3.

12th row: P.2, B.Cr., (k.1 t.b.l., p.1) 4 times, k.1 t.b.l., F.Cr., p.2.

These 12 rows form the pattern.

Back

With 4 mm (No. 8: 5) needles, cast on 72 [78:82:88:92:98:102:108:114] sts.

K. 5 [5:5:5:9:9:9:9:9] rows.

Change to 4½ mm (No. 7: 6) needles.

Beginning k. row, continue in st.-st. until back measures 29 [33:38:42:42:42:42:42:43] cm (11½ [13:15:16½:16½:16½:16½:16½:17] in) ending after a p. row. Mark both ends of last row to indicate beginning of armholes. Continue in st.-st. until work measures 44 [49:54:60:61:62:64:66:67] cm (17½ [19¼:21:23½:24:24½:25½:26:26½] in) ending after a p. row.

Shape Shoulders

Cast off 5 [5:5:6:6:7:7:7:8] sts. at beginning of next 8 rows; 4 [7:8:6:7:6:6:8:6] sts. at beginning of next 2 rows.

Cast off remaining 24 [24:26:28:30:30:34:36:38] sts.

Pocket Linings (make 2)

With 4½ mm (No. 7: 6) needles, cast on 27 sts.

Work 9 [9:9:9:12:12:12:12:12] cm (3½ [3½:3½:3½:5:5:5:5:5] in) st.-st. ending after a p. row. Leave sts. on spare needle.

Left Front

With 4 mm (No. 8: 5) needles, cast on 32
[34:36:38:40:42:44:46:48] sts.
K. 5 [5:5:5:9:9:9:9:9] rows.
Inc. row: K. 3 [4:5:6:7:8:9:10:11] sts., (pick up loop between
sts. and k. in back of it, k.2) 13 times, k. to end. 45
[47:49:51:53:55:57:59:61] sts.
Change to 4½ mm (No. 7: 6) needles and continue in st.-st.
with Aran panel, placing sts. thus:
1st row: (wrong side) P. 9 [10:11:12:13:14:15:16:17] sts., k.2,
p.2, Panel A over next 19 sts., p.2, k.2, p. 9
[10:11:12:13:14:15:16:17].
2nd row: K. 9 [10:11:12:13:14:15:16:17], p.2, Tw.2, Panel A
over next 19 sts., Tw.2, p.2, k. to end.
Continue in pattern with Panel A as now set until front
measures 11 [11:11:11:15:15:15:15:15] cm (4½
[4½:4½:4½:6:6:6:6:6] in) ending after a wrong side row.

Place Pocket

Next row: K. 9 [10:11:12:13:14:15:16:17] sts., slip next 27 sts.
on to stitch holder or spare needle, pattern across 27 sts. of
one pocket lining, k. to end.
Continue in pattern until front is 6 rows less than back to
armhole markers, ending after a wrong side row.

Shape Front

Next row: Keeping pattern correct, pattern to last 2 sts., k. 2
tog. Work 1 row. Repeat last 2 rows twice more. Mark last
row to indicate beginning of armhole.
Now dec. at front edge on next row and every following 2nd
[2nd:2nd:2nd:2nd:3rd:3rd:3rd:3rd:3rd] row until 34
[35:36:37:38:39:40:41:42] sts. remain.
Work straight until front matches back to shoulder, ending
after a wrong side row.

Shape Shoulder

Cast off 7 [7:7:8:8:8:8:9:9] sts. at beginning of next row and
following 3 alternate rows; 6 [7:8:5:6:7:8:5:6] sts. at
beginning of following alternate row.

Right Front

Work as left front, reversing shapings.

Sleeves

With 4 mm (No. 8: 5) needles, cast on 52
[54:56:58:60:60:64:68:70] sts.
K. 5 [5:5:5:9:9:9:9:9] rows.
Inc. row: (right side) K. 8 [9:10:11:3:3:5:7:8], *inc. as for left
front, k. 2 [2:2:2:3:3:3:3:3]; rep. from * 17 times more, inc.
again, k. to end. 71 [73:75:77:79:79:83:87:89] sts.
Change to 4½ mm (No. 7: 6) needles and continue in pattern
placing Panel A thus:
1st row: (wrong side) P. 22 [23:24:25:26:26:28:30:31], k.2,
p.2, Panel A over next 19 sts., p.2, k.2, P. 22
[23:24:25:26:26:28:30:31].

96 *Easy knit jacket, pattern 9*

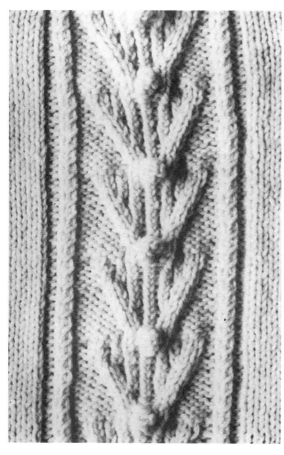

97 *Detail of panel on easy knit jacket,*
pattern 9

Continue in pattern as now set until sleeve measures 30 [33:36:38:42:43:43:44:46] cm (11¾ [13:15:16:16½:17:17:17½:18] in).
Cast off.

Borders and Collar

Join shoulder seams.
With 4 mm (No. 8: 5) needles, cast on 11 sts.
Continue in garter stitch (every row k.) slipping the first st. of 2nd row then every following row, until the border, slightly stretched, fits front edge to beginning of neck shaping.

Shape for Collar

Inc. 1 st. at beginning of next row and at same edge on every following 3rd row to 22 [22:22:22:30:30:30:30:30] sts.
Continue straight until shaped edge of collar fits neck shaping edge to shoulder, ending at straight edge.
Next 2 rows: Slip 1, k. to last 11 sts., turn, k. to end.
Next 2 rows: Slip 1, k. to end.
Repeat last 4 rows until shaped edge fits to centre back neck.
Cast off.
Work the other border and collar piece to correspond.

Pocket Tops

Slip the sts. from one pocket front on to 4 mm (No. 8: 5) needles.
K. 1 row, dec. 5 sts. evenly across.
Work 3 [3:3:3:8:8:8:8:8] rows more in garter stitch.
Cast off sts. loosely.

Belt

With 4 mm (No. 8: 5) needles, cast on 11 sts.
Work in garter stitch as front band until belt measures 86 [91:97:102:107:112:117:122:127] cm (34 [36:38:40:42:44:46:48:50] in).
Cast off sts.

To Make Up

Sew cast off edge of sleeves between armhole markers of fronts and back. Join side and sleeve seams. Sew down pocket linings and pocket borders. Sew on front borders and join shaped edge of collar to front neck, easing round to centre back. Join centre back collar seam.
Press seams.

PATTERN 10: MAN'S ZIP-FRONTED JACKET

Panels of Trinity stitch outlined with twisted rib are used to make an interesting fabric for this easy to knit popular style.

Materials

950 [1000:1050] g Patons Capstan
A pair each 3¾ mm and 4½ mm (No. 9 and No. 7 UK: 4 and 6

USA) knitting needles
60 [60:65] cm (24 [24:26] in) zip fastener

Measurements
To fit 97 [102:107] cm (38 [40:42] in) chest; length, 65
[69:71] cm (25¾ [27:28] in); sleeve seam, 46 [48:51] cm (18
[19:20] in).

Tension
19 sts. to 10 cm (4 in) over stocking stitch

Special Abbreviation
Tw.2, twist 2 thus: k. 2 tog. leaving sts. on left hand needle,
then k. first of these 2 sts. and slip both loops off together.

Back
With 3¾ mm (No. 9: 4) needles, cast on 111 [119:127] sts.
1st row: K.2, *p.1, k.1; rep. from * to last st., k.1.
2nd row: K.1, *p.1, k.1; rep. from * to end.
Repeat last 2 rows 7 times more, then 1st row once.
Inc. row: K. 7 [11:15] sts., *k. twice in next st., k.5; rep. from
* 15 times more, k. twice in next st., k. to end. 128 [136:144]
sts.
Change to 4½ mm (No. 7: 6) needles and continue in pattern
placing sts. thus:
1st row: (right side) K.1, p.2, (k.2, p.2) 4 [5:6] times, p.32,
(p.2, k.2) 6 times, p.2, p.32, (p.2, k.2) 4 [5:6] times, p.2, k.1.
2nd row: K.3, (p.2, k.2) 4 [5:6] times, *(p. 3 tog., k.1-p.1-k.1
all in next st.) 8 times*, (k.2, p.2) 6 times, k.2, rep. from
* to *, (k.2, p.2) 4 [5:6] times, k.3.
3rd row: K.1, p.2, (Tw.2, p.2) 4 [5:6] times, p.32, (p.2, Tw.2)
6 times, p.2, p.32, (p.2, Tw.2) 4 [5:6] times, p.2, k.1.
4th row: K.3, (p.2, k.2) 4 [5:6] times, *(k.1-p.1-k.1 all in next
st., p. 3 tog.) 8 times*, (k.2, p.2) 6 times, k.2, rep. from
* to *, (k.2, p.2) 4 [5:6] times, k.3.
These 4 rows form the pattern.
Continue in pattern as now set until work measures 43
[45:47] cm (17 [17½:18] in), ending after a 4th pattern row.

Shape Armholes
Cast off 8 [12:12] sts. at beginning of next 2 rows. 112
[112:120] sts.
Continue in pattern until armholes measure 18 [19:20] cm (7
[7½:8] in) ending after a wrong side row.

Shape Shoulder Edges
Cast off 10 [10:11] sts. at beginning of next 6 rows; 8 sts. at
beginning of next 2 rows. Leave remaining 36 [36:38] sts. on
spare needle.

Left Front
With 3¾ mm (No. 9: 4) needles, cast on 61 [65:69] sts.
Work 17 rows rib as back welt.
Inc. row: K.4, and slip these 4 sts. on to safety-pin for front
border, k. 4 [6:8] sts., *k. twice in next st., k.5; rep. from * 7
times more, k. twice in next st., k. 4 [6:8]. 66 [70:74] sts.

Change to 4½ mm (No. 7: 6) needles and continue in pattern placing sts. thus:

1st row: K.1, p.2, (k.2, p.2) 4 [5:6] times, p.32, (p.2, k.2) 3 times, p.2, k.1.

Continue in pattern as now set, working the 32 sts. in Trinity pattern with Tw.2, p.2 rib on each side, as back, until front matches back to armhole, ending after a wrong side row.

Shape Armhole

Cast off 8 [12:12] sts. at beginning of next row. 58 [58:62] sts. Continue straight in pattern until armhole measures 16 [16:18] cm (6¼ [6¼:7] in) ending at front edge. These measurements allow for standard zip fastener length; the measurement is approximate to accommodate individual row tension but work should end 12 rows less than back to shoulder.

Shape Neck and Shoulder Edge

Cast off 6 [6:7] sts. at beginning (neck edge) of next row and 4 sts. at same edge on following 2 alternate rows, ending at side edge.

Next row: Cast off 10 [10:11] sts., pattern to end.

Next row: Cast off 2 sts., pattern to end.

Repeat last 2 rows twice more. Cast off remaining 8 sts.

Right Front

As left front, reversing shapings and working inc. row thus:

Inc. row: K. 4 [6:8] sts., *k. twice in next st., k.5; rep. from * 7 times more, k. twice in next st., k. 4 [6:8] sts., turn and slip remaining 4 sts. on to safety-pin for border. 66 [70:74] sts. Place pattern thus:

1st row: K.1, p.2, (k.2, p.2) 3 times, p.32, (p.2, k.2) 4 [5:6] times, p.2, k.1.

Sleeves

With 3¾ mm (No. 9: 4) needles, cast on 47 [49:51] sts. Work 19 rows rib as back welt.

Inc. row: K. 5 [6:7] sts., *k. twice in next st., k.5; rep. from * 5 times more, k. twice in next st., k. to end. 54 [56:58] sts. Change to 4½ mm (No. 7: 6) needles and continue in pattern placing sts. thus:

1st row: (right side) K. 1 [2:3] sts., p.2, (k.2, p.2) 3 times, p.24, (p.2, k.2) 3 times, p.2, k.1 [2:3].

Continue in pattern as now set, working centre 24 sts. in Trinity pattern and remaining sts. in Tw.2, p.2 rib, *at the same time*, inc. 1 st. at both ends of 5th row following and every following 4th row to 90 [94:98] sts. Work inc. sts. into Tw.2, p.2 rib where possible but keeping k.1 at both ends of every row.

Continue straight until sleeve measures 46 [48:51] cm (18 [19:20] in), ending after a 4th pattern row.

Mark both ends of last row. Work 10 [14:14] rows more.

Shape Top

Cast off 4 [6:8] sts. at beginning of next 2 rows; 4 sts. at

beginning of following 16 rows. 18 sts.
Working k.1 at both ends of every row, continue on
remaining sts. in Trinity pattern until extension, slightly
stretched, fits across shaped shoulder edge of back and front.
Leave sts. on spare needle.

98 *Man's zip-fronted jacket,*
pattern 10

Front Borders
Slip sts. of one border on to 3¾ mm (No. 9: 4) needle, cast on

99 *Detail of pattern on zip-fronted jacket, pattern 10*

1 st. at inner edge and continue in rib as back welt until border, slightly stretched, fits front edge to beginning of neck shaping. Leave sts. on spare needle. Work second border in the same way.

To Make Up

Join side edges of sleeve extensions to cast off sts. at shoulders on back and fronts.

Join cast off sts. at top of sleeve to armhole edge, sewing rows above sleeve markers to cast off sts. at underarm.

Join side and sleeve seams. Sew on front borders.

Collar

With right side of work facing, using 3¾ mm (No. 9: 4) needles, cast off 2 sts., (1 st. on right hand needle), rib 2, pick up and k. 18 [18:20] sts. up right front neck edge, k. 18 sts. from sleeve extension, k. 36 [36:38] sts. from back neck, k. 18 sts. from sleeve extension, pick up and k. 18 [18:20] sts. from left front neck edge, rib 3, cast off 2 sts. 114 [114:120] sts.

Rejoin yarn and work 5 cm (2 in) k.1, p.1 rib.

Cast off sts. loosely in rib.

Press work lightly, avoiding ribbed sections.

Fold collar in half to wrong side and slip stitch.

Sew in zip fastener.

PATTERN 11: CHILD'S ARAN PATTERNED COAT

A chevron pattern forms the panel between the twist stitch ribs and Irish moss on this warm coat for little girls.

Matching hat and mitts are on pages 113 and 114 (patterns 12 and 13).

100 *Detail of panels on child's coat, hat and mitts, patterns, 12 and 13*

Materials

500 [550:600] g Emu Aran yarn
A pair 4½ mm (No. 7 UK: 6 USA) knitting needles
A cable needle
3 medium buttons
1 small button

Measurements

To fit 61 [66:71] cm (24 [26:28] in) chest; length, 45 [51:57]
cm (17¾ [20:22½] in); sleeve seam, 24 [29:35] cm (9¾ [11½:13¾]
in)

Tension

19 sts. to 10 cm (4 in) over stocking stitch

Special Abbreviations

R.Tw., right twist thus: k. second st. on left hand needle,
then k. first st. and slip both loops off together.
L.Tw., left twist thus: k. t.b.l. second st. on left hand needle,
then k. first st. and slip both loops off together.
C. 4 F., cable 4 front thus: slip next 2 sts. to front on cable
needle, k.2, then k.2 from cable needle.
B.Cr., back cross thus: slip next st. to back on cable needle,
k.2, then p.1 from cable needle.
F.Cr., front cross thus: slip next 2 sts. to front on cable
needle, p.1, then k.2 from cable needle.
D.M. stitch, double moss stitch thus:
1st row: K.1, *p.1, k.1; rep. from * to end.
2nd row: P.1, *k.1, p.1; rep. from * to end.
3rd row: As 2nd row.
4th row: As 1st row.
These 4 rows form the pattern.

Panel A   Chevron pattern 26 sts.

1st row: (right side) K.1 t.b.l., p.1, R.Tw., L.Tw., p.1, *p.4,
C. 4 F.*, p.1, R.Tw., L.Tw., p.1, k.1 t.b.l.
2nd row: P.1, k.1, p.4, k.1, *k.4, p.4, k.4*, k.1, p.4, k.1, p.1.
3rd row: K.1 t.b.l., p.1, R.Tw., L.Tw., p.1, *p.3, B.Cr.,
F.Cr., p.3*, p.1, R.Tw., L.Tw., p.1, k.1 t.b.l.
4th row and following wrong side rows: K. the k. sts. and p.
the p. sts. as they present themselves.
5th row: K.1 t.b.l., p.1, R.Tw., L.Tw., p.1, *p.2, B.Cr., p.2,
F.Cr., p.2*, p.1, R.Tw., L.Tw., p.1, k.1 t.b.l.
7th row: K.1 t.b.l., p.1, R.Tw., L.Tw., p.1, *p.1, B.Cr., p.4,
F.Cr., p.1*, p.1, R.Tw., L.Tw., p.1, k.1 t.b.l.
9th row: K.1 t.b.l., p.1, R.Tw., L.Tw., p.1, *B.Cr., p.1, C. 4
F., p.1, F.Cr.*, p.1, R.Tw., L.Tw., p.1, k.1 t.b.l.
10th row: As 4th row.
Repeat 3rd to 10th rows for pattern.

Back

With 4½ mm (No. 7: 6) needles, cast on 81 [85:89] sts.
Continue in pattern, placing panels thus:
Next row: (wrong side) D.M. stitch over 11 sts., **p.1, k.1,

p.4, k.5, p.4, k.5, p.4, k.1, p.1**, D.M. stitch over centre 7 [11:15] sts., repeat from ** to **, D.M. stitch over last 11 sts.

1st row: D.M. stitch over next 11 sts., Panel A over next 26 sts., D.M. stitch over centre 7 [11:15] sts., Panel A over next 26 sts., D.M. stitch over 11 sts.

Now continue in pattern with panels as set until work measures 10 cm (4 in), ending after a wrong side row.

Dec. 1 st. at both ends of next row and following 8th rows until 69 [73:77] sts. remain.

Keeping pattern correct, continue straight until work measures 31 [35:40] cm (12¼ [13¾:15¾] in), ending after a wrong side row.

Shape Armholes

Cast off 3 sts. at beginning of next 2 rows. Dec. 1 st. at both ends of next row and following alternate rows to 59 [63:67] sts. Continue straight until armholes measure 14 [16:17] cm (5½ [6¼:6¾] in), ending after a wrong side row.

Shape Shoulders

Cast off 10 [11:12] sts. at beginning of next 2 rows; 10 [10:11] sts. at beginning of following 2 rows. Leave remaining 19 [21:21] sts. on spare needle.

Left Front

With 4½ mm (No. 7: 6) needles, cast on 47 [49:51] sts.
Continue in pattern placing sts. thus:
Next row: (wrong side) D.M. stitch over 10 [12:14] sts., work 2nd row of Panel A over next 26 sts., D.M. stitch over 11 sts.
1st row: D.M. stitch over 11 sts., work 1st row of Panel A over 26 sts., D.M. stitch to end.
2nd row: D.M. stitch over 10 [12:14] sts., work 2nd row of Panel A over 26 sts., D.M. stitch to end.
Continue in pattern with panel as now set, repeating 3rd to 10th rows of Panel A between D.M. stitch until work measures 10 cm (4 in) ending after a wrong side row.

Shape Side

Dec. 1 st. at beginning of next row and following 8th rows to 41 [43:45] sts. Continue straight until work matches back to armhole, ending after a wrong side row.

Shape Armhole

Cast off 3 sts. at beginning of next row. Dec. 1 st. at beginning of following alternate rows to 36 [38:40] sts. Continue straight until armhole measures 9 [11:12] cm (3½ [4¼:4¾] in), ending after a right side row.

Shape Neck

Cast off 9 [10:10] sts. at beginning of next row; 3 sts. at beginning of following alternate row. Dec. 1 st. at neck edge on every row until 20 [21:23] sts. remain. Continue straight until armhole matches back to shoulder, ending after a wrong side row.

101 OPPOSITE *Child's Aran patterned coat, hat and mitts, patterns 11, 12 and 13*

Shape Shoulder

Cast off 10 [11:12] sts. at beginning of next row; 10 [10:11] sts. at beginning of following alternate row.

Right Front

Work as left front, reversing shapings; having D.M. stitch over 11 sts. at beginning of pattern placing row and at end of right side pattern rows.

For buttonholes, mark left front with pins to represent. buttons, the top one to be 4 cm (1½ in) below beginning of neck shaping, the remaining two to be spaced each 5 [6:7] cm (2 [2½:2¾] in) below.

When working right front, work buttonholes to correspond with pinned positions thus:

1st buttonhole row: (right side) D.M. stitch over 2 sts., cast off 3 sts., pattern to end.

2nd row: In pattern, casting on 3 sts. over those cast off in previous row.

Sleeves

With 4½ mm (No. 7: 6) needles, cast on 34 [38:46] sts.

Next row: D.M. stitch over 4 [6:10] sts., work 2nd row of Panel A over next 26 sts., D.M. stitch over 4 [6:10] sts.

1st pattern row: D.M. stitch over 4 [6:10] sts., work 1st row of Panel A over next 26 sts., D.M. stitch to end.

Continue in pattern as now set, inc. 1 st. at both ends of 7th row and every following 6th row to 50 [54:62] sts., working inc. sts. in to D.M. stitch.

Continue in pattern until sleeve measures 24 [29:35] cm (9¾ [11½:13¾] in), ending after a wrong side row.

Shape Top

Cast off 3 sts. at beginning of next 2 rows. Dec. 1 st. at both ends of next row and following alternate rows to 34 [38:40] sts. ending after a wrong side row.

Dec. 1 st. at both ends of next 8 [10:10] rows.

Cast off remaining 18 [18:20] sts.

Collar

With 4½ mm (No. 7: 6) needles, cast on 75 [82:89] sts.

1st row: (right side) P.2, k.1 t.b.l., *p.1, k.4, p.1, k.1 t.b.l.; rep. from * to last 2 sts., p.2.

2nd row: K.2, p.1, *k.1, p.4, k.1, p.1; rep. from * to last 2 sts., k.2.

3rd row: P.2, k.1 t.b.l., *p.1, R.Tw., L.Tw., p.1, k.1 t.b.l.; rep. from * to last 2 sts., p.2.

Repeat 2nd and 3rd rows until work measures 5 [6:7] cm (2 [2½:2¾] in) ending after a wrong side row and dec. 1 st. at centre on 2nd size only. 75 [81:89] sts.

Shape Back Neck

1st row: K.2, *p.1, k.1; rep. from * to last st., k.1.

2nd row: k.1, *p.1, k.1; rep. from * to end.

Keeping rib correct as now set, shape thus:

Next 2 rows: Rib to last 6 sts., turn.

Next 2 rows: Rib to last 12 sts., turn.
Continue in this way, working 6 sts. less before turning until the 2 rows 'rib to last 30 sts., turn' have been worked, rib to end.
Work 1 row rib across all sts.
Cast off all sts. loosely in rib.

To Make Up

Press pieces lightly.
Join shoulder seams. Join side and sleeve seams. Sew in sleeves. Sew on collar. Sew on buttons. Work small loop at corner of neck shaping and sew small button to correspond under collar edge. Press seams.

PATTERN 12: CHILD'S HAT

An Aran patterned hat to match the coat, pattern 11, on page 108.

Materials

100g Emu Aran yarn
A pair 4½ mm (No. 7 UK: 6 USA knitting needles
A cable needle

Measurement

To fit average head size.

Tension

19 sts. to 10 cm (4 in) over stocking stitch

Special Abbreviations

As pattern 11, see page 108.

To Make

With 4½ mm (No. 7: 6) needles, cast on 93 sts.
1st row: K.2, *p.1, k.1; rep. from * to last st., k.1.
2nd row: K.1, *p.1, k.1; rep. from * to end.
Repeat last 2 rows twice more, then 1st row once.
Inc. row: Inc. in 1st st., *rib 8, inc. in next st.; rep. from * 9 times more, inc. in next st., k.1. 105 sts.
Next row: (wrong side) K.1, (k.1, p.1, k.1, work from * to * on 2nd row of Panel A, k.1 p.1) 6 times, k.2.
Now continue in pattern, placing sts. thus:
1st row: (right side) P.1, (p.1, k.1 t.b.l., p.1, work from * to * on 1st row of Panel A, p.1, k.1 t.b.l.) 6 times, p.2.
Repeat 2nd to 10th rows, working from * to * of Panel A then 3rd to 10th rows only.
Next row: P.1, (p.1, k.1 t.b.l., p.5, k.1 t.b.l., p.2, k.1 t.b.l., p.5, k.1 t.b.l.) 6 times, p.2.
Next row: K.1, (k.1, p.1, k.5, p.1, k.1, p.1, k.5, p.1) 6 times, k.2.
Repeat last 2 rows twice more.

Shape Crown

1st row: P.1, (p.1, k.1 t.b.l., p. 2 tog., p.1, p. 2 tog., k.1 t.b.l., p.2, k.1 t.b.l., p. 2 tog., p.1, p. 2 tog., k.1 t.b.l.) 6 times, p.2.

Next 3 rows: K. the k. sts. and p. the p. sts. as they present themselves.

5th row: P.1, (p.1, k.1 t.b.l., p. 3 tog., k.1 t.b.l., p.2, k.1 t.b.l., p. 3 tog., k.1 t.b.l.) 6 times, p.2 tog.

Next 3 rows: K. the k. sts. and p. the p. sts. as they present themselves.

9th row: P.1, (k. 2 tog. t.b.l., p.1 k.1 t.b.l., p. 2 tog., k.1 t.b.l., k. 2 tog.) 6 times, p.1. 38 sts.

Next row: (K. 2 tog.) 19 times.

Next row: (P. 2 tog.) to last st., p.1.
sts. Draw up and secure tightly.

To Make Up

Press lightly avoiding ribbed brim.

Using long end, join back seam. With remaining yarn, make a pom-pom and sew to centre of crown.

PATTERN 13: CHILD'S MITTS

Cosy mitts to match the coat and hat of patterns 11 and 12, pages 108 and 113.

Materials

100g Emu Aran yarn
A pair each 3¾ mm and 4½ mm (No. 9 and No. 7 UK: 4 and 6 USA) knitting needles
A cable needle

Measurements

To fit 12.5 cm (5 in) wrist to finger tip (adjustable).

Tension

19 sts. to 10 cm (4 in) over stocking stitch

Special Abbreviations and Pattern Panel

As pattern 11 (see page 108).

To Make

With 3¾ mm (No. 9: 4) needles, cast on 29 sts.
Work 10 rows rib thus:

1st row: K.2, *p.1, k.1; rep. from * to last st., k.1.

2nd row: K.1, *p.1, k.1; rep. from * to end.

On 10th rib row inc. 1 st. at beginning of row for first mitt and at end of row for second mitt.

Change to 4½ mm (No. 7: 6) needles.

Next row: K.1, pattern from * to * on 2nd row of Panel A over next 12 sts., p.4, pattern from * to * on 2nd row of Panel A over next 12 sts., k.1.

Now continue in pattern thus:

1st row: K.1, pattern from * to * of 1st row of Panel A over next 12 sts., k.4, pattern from * to * of 1st row of Panel A over next 12 sts., k.1.

2nd row: As set, working from * to * of 2nd row of Panel A over 12 sts. between st.-st.

Shape for Thumb

3rd row: K.1, pattern from * to * of 3rd row of Panel A over next 12 sts., inc. in next st., k.1, inc. in next st., k.1, pattern from * to * of 3rd row of Panel A over next 12 sts., k.1.

4th row: As set, working from * to * of 4th row of Panel A over 12 sts., between st.-st.

5th row: K.1, pattern from * to * of 5th row of Panel A over 12 sts., k.6, pattern from * to * of Panel A over 12 sts., k.1.

6th row: As 4th row.

7th row: K.1, pattern from * to * of 7th row of Panel A over 12 sts., inc. in next st., k.3, inc. in next st., k.1, pattern from * to * of 7th row of Panel A over 12 sts., k.1.

Continue in this manner, inc. on every 4th row to 36 sts. Work 1 row.

Thumb

Next row: Pattern 22 sts., turn. Cast on 1 st., turn, k.1, p.8, cast on 1 st., turn. Work 8 rows st.-st. on these 10 sts.

Next row: (K. 2 tog.) to end.

P. 1 row.

Break yarn, thread end through remaining sts., draw up and secure. With 14 sts. on right hand needle, pick up and k. 1 st. from each side of base of thumb, then work remaining 14 sts. Continue in pattern on remaining 30 sts. until 28 pattern rows in all have been worked. Length may be adjusted here.

Shape Top

Next row: (K.1, slip 1, k.1, p.s.s.o., pattern 9, k. 2 tog., k.1) twice.

Work 1 row.

3rd row: (K.1, slip 1, k.1, p.s.s.o., pattern 7, k. 2 tog., k.1) twice.

Continue dec. in the same way until 14 sts. remain.

Cast off sts.

Work a second mitt in the same manner, reversing shapings.

To Make Up

Press lightly, avoiding cuff rib. Join side and thumb seams.

PATTERN 14: CHILD'S SWEATER WITH CROSSOVER SHAWL COLLAR

A raglan sweater for outdoor wear, quickly made in stocking stitch with cable panels and an unusual diamond cable pattern.

Materials

240 [280:320] g Wendy Aran machine washable yarn
A pair each 3¾ mm and 4½ mm (No. 9 and No. 7 UK: 4 and 6 USA) knitting needles
A cable needle

Measurements

To fit 56 [61:66] cm (22 [24:26] in) chest; length, 34 [38:42] cm (13½ [15:16½] in); sleeve seam, 26 [30:33] cm (10¼ [11¾:13] in)

102 *Child's sweater with crossover shawl collar, pattern 14*

Tension
19 sts. to 10 cm (4 in) over stocking stitch

Special Abbreviations
C. 9, cable 9 sts. thus: slip next st. to front on cable needle, k.3, then k.1 from cable needle, k.1, slip next 3 sts. to back on cable needle, k.1, then k.3 from cable needle.
C. 6 F., cable 6 front thus: slip next 3 sts. to front on cable needle, k.3, then k.3 from cable needle.
C. 6 B., cable 6 back thus: slip next 3 sts. to back on cable needle, k.3, then k.3 from cable needle.
C. 6 B.P., cable 6 back purl thus: slip next 3 sts. to back on cable needle, k.3, then p.3 from cable needle.

C. 6 F.P., cable 6 front purl thus: slip next 3 sts. to front on cable needle, p.3, then k.3 from cable needle.

Panel A   Gull Stitch 9 sts.
1st row: K.
2nd row: P.
3rd row: C. 9.
4th row: P.
These 4 rows form the pattern.

Panel B   Diamond and Step Cable Pattern 22 sts.
1st row: P.8, k.6, p.8.
2nd row and foll. alt. rows: K. the k. sts. and p. the p. sts. as they present themselves.
3rd row: As 1st row.
5th row: P.5, k.3, C. 6 F., k.3, p.5.
7th row: P.5, k.12, p.5.
9th row: As 7th row.
11th row: P.2, k.3, C. 6 B.P., C. 6 F.P., k.3, p.2.
13th row: P.2, k.6, p.6, k.6, p.2.
15th row: As 13th row.
17th row: P.2, C. 6 B.P., p.6, C. 6 F.P., p.2.
19th row: P.2, k.3, p.12, k.3, p.2.
21st row: As 19th row.
23rd row: P.2, C. 6 F., p.6, C. 6 B., p.2.
25th and 27th rows: As 13th row.
29th row: P.5, C. 6 F., C. 6 B., p.5.
31st and 33rd rows: As 7th row.
35th row: P.8, C. 6 F., P.8.
36th row: K.8, p.6, k.8.
These 36 rows form the pattern.

Panel C   Six-Stitch Cable 6 sts.
1st row: (right side) K.
2nd row: P.
3rd row: C. 6 F.
4th row: P.
5th to 8th rows: Rep. 1st and 2nd rows twice.
These 8 rows form the pattern.

Back
With 3¾ mm (No. 9: 4) needles, cast on 70 [76:82] sts.
Work 10 rows k.1, p.1 rib.
Change to 4½ mm (No. 7: 6) needles and continue in panels of stocking stitch and cable thus:
1st row: (right side) K. 13 [16:19], p.2, Panel A over next 9 sts., Panel B over next 22 sts., Panel A over next 9 sts., p.2, K. 13 [16:19].
2nd row: P. 13 [16:19], k.2, Panel A over next 9 sts., Panel B over next 22 sts., Panel A over next 9 sts., k.2, p. 13 [16:19].
Continue with pattern in panels as now set until work measures 21 [24:27] cm (8½ [9½:10¾] in), ending after a wrong side row.**

103 *Detail of panel on child's sweater,*
pattern 14

Shape Raglan

Cast off 2 [3:2] sts. at beginning of next 2 rows. Dec. 1 st. at both ends of every row until 58 [66:66] sts. remain. Now dec. 1 st. at both ends of next 2 rows, then work 1 row straight. Repeat last 3 rows until 18 sts. remain. Leave sts. on spare needle.

Front

Work as back to **.

Shape Raglan

Work as back raglan shaping until 58 [66:66] sts. remain. Dec. 1 st. at both ends of next 2 rows.

Divide for Neck

Next row: Pattern 18 [22:22] sts., cast off centre 18 sts. loosely, pattern to end.

Work on first set of sts. for right side of neck, dec. at side edge on next 2 rows, then work 1 row straight. Repeat last 3 rows until all sts. are worked off.

Join yarn to remaining sts. and complete this side to match right side, reversing shapings.

Sleeves

With $3\frac{3}{4}$ mm (No. 9: 4) needles, cast on 36 [38:40] sts.
Work 10 rows k.1, p.1 rib, inc. 4 sts. evenly across last row. 40 [42:44] sts.

Change to $4\frac{1}{2}$ mm (No. 7: 6) needles and work in pattern, placing sts. thus:

1st row: (right side) K. 4 [5:6] sts., p.2, Panel A over 9 sts., p.2, Panel C over 6 sts., p.2, Panel A over 9 sts., p.2, k. 4 [5:6] sts.

2nd row: P. 4 [5:6] sts., k.2, Panel A over 9 sts., k.2, Panel C over 6 sts., k.2, Panel A over 9 sts., k.2, p. 4 [5:6].

Continue in pattern with panels as now set, inc. 1 st. at both ends of 9th row following and every following 4th row to 58 [64:70] sts., working inc. sts. in st.-st.

Continue straight until sleeve measures 26 [30:33] cm ($10\frac{1}{4}$ [$11\frac{3}{4}$:13] in) ending after a wrong side row.

Shape Raglan

Cast off 2 [3:2] sts. at beginning of next 2 rows. Dec. 1 st. at both ends of every row until 46 [54:54] sts. remain. Dec. 1 st. at both ends of next 2 rows, then work 1 row straight. Repeat last 3 rows until 6 sts. remain. Leave sts. on spare needle.

Collar

Join raglan seams.

With right side of work facing, using three $3\frac{3}{4}$ mm (No. 9: 4) needles, pick up and k. 28 [34:34] sts. along right front neck edge, k. sts. from one sleeve top, k. sts. from back neck inc. in every alternate st., k. sts. from second sleeve top, pick up and k. 29 [35:35] sts. along left front neck edge. 96 [108:108] sts.

Work 8 cm ($3\frac{1}{4}$ in) k.1, p.1 rib.
Cast off sts. loosely in rib.

To Make Up

Join side and sleeve seams. Sew edges of collar to cast off edges of centre front, lapping right side over left for girl's sweater and left over right for boy's sweater.

Press seams, avoiding ribbed sections.

PATTERN 15: LADY'S FULL LENGTH ARAN PATTERNED COAT

Bobble fan pattern, Trinity pattern and Irish moss form the panels of a coat that looks smart in town and country alike.

Materials

1200 [1240:1280:1320:1360] g Wendy Aran machine washable yarn

A pair each 3¼ mm and 4½ mm (No. 10 and No. 7 UK: 3 and 6 USA) knitting needles

A cable needle

4·5 mm crochet hook

5 buttons

Measurements

To fit 81 [86:91:97:102] cm (32 [34:36:38:40] in) bust; length, 94 [95:96:97:98] cm (37 [37¼:37¾:38:38½] in); sleeve seam, 44 cm (17½ in)

Tension

19 sts. to 10 cm (4 in) over stocking stitch

Special Abbreviations

R.Tw., right twist thus: k. second st. on left hand needle, then k. first st. and slip both loops off together.

L.Tw., left twist thus: k. t.b.l. second st. on left hand needle, then k. first st. and slip both loops off together.

M.B., make bobble thus: (k.1, y.fwd., k.1, y.fwd., k.1) all in next st., turn and p.5, turn and k.5, turn and p. 2 tog., p.1, p. 2 tog., turn and slip 1, k. 2 tog., p.s.s.o.,—bobble made.

F.Cr., front cross thus: slip next st. to front on cable needle, p.1, then k.1 from cable needle.

B.Cr., back cross thus: slip next st. to back on cable needle, k.1, then p.1 from cable needle.

Panel A   Trinity Pattern 4 sts.

1st row: (right side) P.
2nd row: K.1, p.1, k.1 all in next st., p. 3 tog.
3rd row: P.
4th row: P. 3 tog., k.1, p.1, k.1.
These 4 rows form the pattern.

Panel B   Bobble Fan Pattern 15 sts.

1st row: (right side) P.
2nd row: K.
3rd row: P.7, M.B., p.7.
4th row: K.7, p.1 t.b.l., k.7.
5th row: P.4, M.B., p.2, k.1 t.b.l., p.2, M.B., p.4.

104 *Full length Aran patterned coat, pattern 15*

105 *Detail of panels on full length coat, pattern 15*

6th row: K.4, p.1 t.b.l., k.2, p.1, k.2, p.1 t.b.l., k.4.
7th row: P.2, M.B., p.1, F.Cr., p.1, k.1 t.b.l., p.1, B.Cr., p.1, M.B., p.2.
8th row: K.2, p.1 t.b.l., k.2, (p.1, k.1) 3 times, k.1, p.1 t.b.l., k.2.
9th row: P.2, F.Cr., p.1, F.Cr., k.1 t.b.l., B.Cr., p.1, B.Cr., p.2.
10th row: K.3, B.Cr., k.1, p.3, k.1, F.Cr., k.3.
11th row: P.4, F.Cr., pick up loop between sts. and p. in back of it, slip 1, k.2 tog., p.s.s.o., pick up loop between sts. and p. in back of it, B.Cr., p.4.
12th row: K.5, B.Cr., p.1, F.Cr., k.5.
13th row: P.5, p. in front and back of next st., slip 1, k.2 tog., p.s.s.o., p. in front and back of next st., p.5.
14th row: K.7, p.1, k.7.
15th and 16th rows: As 1st and 2nd rows.
These 16 rows form the pattern.

Panel C Irish Moss Stitch

1st and 2nd rows: K.1, *p.1, k.1; rep. from * to end.
3rd and 4th rows: P.1, *k.1, p.1; rep. from * to end.
These 4 rows form the pattern.

Back Skirt

With 4½ mm (No. 7: 6) needles, cast on 129 [135:141:147:153] sts.
Work in pattern placing panels thus:
1st row: K.1, Panel A over 4 sts., *k.1 t.b.l., Panel B over 15 sts., k.1 t.b.l., p.2, L.Tw., Panel C over 9 [11:13:15:17] sts., R.Tw., p.2*, rep. from * to * twice more, k.1 t.b.l., Panel B over 15 sts., k.1 t.b.l., Panel A over 4 sts., k.1.
2nd row: K.1, Panel A over 4 sts., *p.1, Panel B over 15 sts., p.1, k.2, p.2, Panel C over 9 [11:13:15:17] sts., p.2, k.2*, rep. from * to * twice more, p.1, Panel B over 15 sts., p.1, Panel A over 4 sts., k.1.
3rd row: As 1st row, work R.Tw. in place of L.Tw. and L.Tw. in place of R.Tw.
4th row: As 2nd row.
Continue in pattern, with panels as now set until work measures 23 cm (9 in), ending after a wrong side row.

Shape Irish Moss Panels

Dec. row: K.1, Panel A over 4 sts., *k.1 t.b.l., Panel B over 15 sts., k.1 t.b.l., p.2, Tw.2 in sequence, k. 2 tog., Panel C to within 2 sts. of next Tw.2 sts., k. 2 tog., Tw.2 in sequence, p.2*, rep. from * to * twice more, k.1 t.b.l., Panel B over 15 sts., k.1 t.b.l., Panel A over 4 sts., k.1. 123 [129:135:141:147] sts.
Repeat the dec. row, decreasing 6 sts. each time, when work measures 43 cm (17 in), 59 cm (23 in) and 69 cm (27 in). 105 [111:117:123:129] sts.
Continue straight in pattern with 1 [3:5:7:9] sts. in Panel C between Tw.2 patterns, until work measures 74 cm (29 in),

ending after a wrong side row.
Cast off sts.

Left Front

With 4½ mm (No. 7: 6) needles, cast on 66 [68:70:72:74] sts.
1st row: K.1, Panel A over 4 sts., repeat from * to * on back pattern 1st row, k.1 t.b.l., Panel B over 15 sts., k.1 t.b.l., p.2, L.Tw., k.1, R.Tw., p.2, k.1.
2nd row: K.1, k.2, p.2, p.1, p.2, k.2, p.1, Panel B over 15 sts., p.1, rep. from * to * on back pattern 2nd row, Panel A over 4 sts., k.1.
Note: The k. and p. sts. follow the sequence of pattern.
3rd row: K.1, Panel A over 4 sts., rep. from * to * on 3rd row of back pattern, k.1 t.b.l., Panel B over 15 sts., k.1 t.b.l., p.2, R.Tw., p.1, L.Tw., p.2, k.1.
4th row: K.1, k.2, p.2, k.1, p.2, k.2, p.1, Panel B over 15 sts., p.1, repeat from * to * on back pattern 4th row, Panel A over 4 sts., k.1.
Continue in pattern with panels as now set until work measures 23 cm (9 in), ending after a wrong side row.

Shape Irish Moss Panels

Dec. row: K.1, Panel A over 4 sts., k.1 t.b.l., Panel B over 15 sts., k.1 t.b.l., p.2, Tw.2 in sequence, k. 2 tog., Panel C to within 2 sts. of next Tw.2 sts., k. 2 tog., Tw.2 in sequence, p.2, k.1 t.b.l., Panel B over 15 sts., k.1 t.b.l., p.2, Tw.2 in sequence, Panel C over 1 st., Tw.2 in sequence, p.2, k.1. 64 [66:68:70:72] sts.
Repeat the dec. row, decreasing 2 sts. each time, when work measures 43 cm (17 in), 59 cm (23 in) and 69 cm (27 in). 58 [60:62:64:66] sts.
Continue straight in pattern until work measures 74 cm (29 in) ending after same pattern row as back.
Cast off sts.

Right Front

Work as left front, reversing shapings, placing panels thus:
1st row: K.1, p.2, L.Tw., Pattern C over 1 st., R.Tw., p.2, k.1 t.b.l., Pattern B over 15 sts., k.1 t.b.l., repeat from * to * on back pattern 1st row, Panel A over 4 sts., k.1.

Yoke Back

With 4½ mm (No. 7: 6) needles, cast on 84 [88:92:100:104] sts.
The yoke is worked in Panel A throughout.
Work in Panel A until piece measures 20 [21:22:23:24] cm [8¼:8½:9:9½] in), ending after a wrong side row.

Shape Shoulders

Cast off 28 [28:32:32:36] sts., pattern centre 28 [32:28:36:32] sts., and slip these sts. on spare needle, cast off remaining 28 [28:32:32:36] sts.

Left Front Yoke

With 4½ mm (No. 7: 6) needles, cast on 52 [52:56:56:60] sts.

106 *Long, slim lines emphasize the rich pattern, pattern 15*

107 *Collar and high yoke of the full length coat, pattern 15*

Work in Panel A until yoke measures 12 [13:14:15:16] cm (4¾ [5:5½:6:6¼] in) ending after a 1st pattern row.

Shape Neck

1st row: (wrong side) cast off 12 sts., slip the st. on right hand needle back on to left hand needle and work as 2nd row to end.

2nd row: P. to last 8 sts., (p.2 tog.) to end. 4 sts. dec.

3rd row: As 3rd Panel A row.

4th row: As 2nd dec. row.

5th row: As 1st Panel A row.

6th row: As 2nd dec. row. 28 [28:32:32:36] sts.

Continue straight in pattern until work matches back to shoulder, ending at side edge.

Cast off sts.

Right Front Yoke

Mark left front yoke with pins to represent buttons, the top one to be 4 rows below beginning of neck shaping, the lowest to be 4 rows from cast on edge and the remaining pin placed equally between.

Work the right front yoke to match the left, reversing shapings and working buttonholes to correspond with the pinned positions thus:

1st row: (right side) P.4, cast off 4 sts., p. to end.

2nd row: In pattern, casting on 4 sts. over those cast off in previous row.

The dec. rows of neck shaping should be worked on the right side of the work, working (p.2 tog.) 4 times, at the beginning of shaping rows instead of the end. The pattern will then present itself correctly for the following row.

Sleeves

With 4½ mm (No. 7: 6) needles, cast on 97 [97:105:105:105] sts.

Work in pattern, placing panels thus:

1st row: K.1, Panel A over 4 sts., *p.2, L.Tw., Panel C over 1 [1:3:3:3: sts., R.Tw., p.2, k.1 t.b.l., Panel B over 15 sts., k.1 t.b.l.*, repeat from * to * twice more, p.2, L.Tw., Panel C over 1 [1:3:3:3] sts., R.Tw., p.2, Panel A over 4 sts., k.1.

Continue in pattern with panels as now set until sleeves measure 43 cm (17 in). Mark both ends of last row. Work 5 cm (2 in) more, ending after same pattern row as back and front skirt.

Cast off sts. loosely.

Collar

Join yoke shoulders.

With 4½ mm (No. 7: 6) needles, cast on 19 sts.

Work in Panel B outlined with rib, placing sts. thus:

1st row: K.1, k.1 t.b.l., Panel B over 15 sts., k.1 t.b.l., k.1.

2nd row: K.1, p.1, Panel B over 15 sts., p.1, k.1.

Continue with pattern as now set until collar piece fits round neck edge. Cast off sts.

Neckband

With right side of work facing, using 3¼ mm (No. 10: 3) needles, beginning and ending at front neck edges, pick up and k. 91 [95:99:103:107] sts. evenly round neck edge, including sts. on back neck spare needle.

Beginning and ending next row and following wrong side rows, p.1, continue in k.1, p.1 rib until depth of neckband matches width of collar piece, *at the same time*, working two buttonholes in right neckband as before, the first to be 6 rows from the picked up edge and the last to be 6 rows from the end.

Cast off sts. in rib.

To Make Up

With right side of work facing, work 1 row double crochet round all edges of yoke, working 3 d.c. in each corner. *Do not turn*; work 1 row shrimp stitch all round the d.c. row. (Shrimp stitch is double crochet worked from left to right.) Fasten off. Join cast off edge of back skirt to lower edge of back yoke, leaving approximately 5 cm (2 in) of skirt extending at each side and lapping the shrimp stitch edge of the yoke over the cast off edge of the skirt. Join cast off edges of the two fronts to the yoke fronts in the same way.

Sew cast off edge of sleeves to armhole edges, lapping the shrimp stitch border to conceal the seams, and sewing rows above markers to side extensions of the front and back skirt. Join sleeve seams. Join side seams leaving 18 cm (7 in) open at lower edge. With right side of work facing, work 1 row double crochet round all outer edges of skirt, including the side-slits, working 3 d.c. in each corner. *Do not turn*; work 1 row shrimp stitch along the d.c. row. Fasten off.

Work 1 row double crochet then 1 row shrimp stitch round sleeve edges.

With right side of work facing, work 1 row double crochet then 1 row shrimp stitch round collar piece.

Sew on collar piece over neckband.

Sew on buttons; the top two buttons will be concealed in fastening behind the collar piece.

Press work lightly.

PATTERN 16: LADY'S EVENING WAISTCOAT

Traditional Aran patterns combined with a luxury yarn can transform a useful everyday garment into a glamorous evening accessory.

Materials

225 [250:275:300:325:350] g Twilley Goldfingering
A pair each 3 mm and 3¼ mm (No. 11 and No. 10 UK: 2 and 3 USA) knitting needles
A cable needle
8 buttons

Measurements

To fit 81 [86:91:97:102:107] cm (32 [34:36:38:40:42] in) bust; length, 53 [54:55:55:58:58] cm (20¾ [21:21½:21½:22¾:22¾] in)

Tension

32 sts. to 10 cm (4 in) over pattern
28 sts. to 10 cm (4 in) over stocking stitch

Special Abbreviations

F.Cr., front cross thus: slip next 2 sts. to front on cable needle, p.1, then k.2 from cable needle.
B.Cr., back cross thus: slip next st. to back on cable needle, k.2, then p.1 from cable needle.
C. 4 F., cable 4 front thus: slip next 2 sts. to front on cable needle, k.2, then k.2 from cable needle.
C. 4 B., cable 4 back thus: slip next 2 sts. to back on cable needle, k.2, then k.2 from cable needle.

Panel A   Trinity Pattern 4 sts.

1st row: (right side) P.
2nd row: K.1, p.1, k.1 all in next st., p.3 tog.
3rd row: P.
4th row: P.3 tog., k.1, p.1, k.1 all in next st.
These 4 rows form the pattern.

Panel B   Twist Stitch Rib 4 sts.

1st row: P.2, k. second st. on left hand needle, then k. first st. and slip both loops off together—called Tw.2 K.
2nd row: P. second st. on left hand needle, then p. first st. and slip both loops off together—called Tw.2 P., k.2.
These 2 rows form the pattern.

Panel C   Aran Honeycomb 8 sts.

1st row: (right side) K.
2nd row and foll. alt. rows: P.
3rd row: C. 4 F., C. 4 B.
5th row: K.
7th row: C. 4 B., C. 4 F.
8th row: As 2nd row.
These 8 rows form the pattern.

Panel D   Zigzag and Bobble Pattern 14 sts.

1st row: (right side) P.3, k.2, p.9.
2nd row and foll. alt. rows: K. the k. sts. and p. the p. sts. as they present themselves.
3rd row: P.3, F.Cr., p.8.
5th row: P.4, F.Cr., p.7.
7th row: P.5, F.Cr., p.6.
9th row: P.6, F.Cr., p.5.
11th row: P.7, F.Cr., p.4.
13th row: P.5, p.1 leaving loop on left hand needle, k. into front and back of same loop 4 times more, then drop loop (thus making 5 sts. out of 1 st.) p.2, F.Cr., p.3.
14th row: K.3, p.2, k.3, p.5, k.5.
15th row: P.5, slip next 5 sts. on to right hand needle, yarn

108 OPPOSITE *Lady's evening waistcoat, pattern 16*

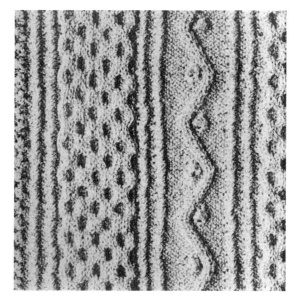

109 *Detail of panels on gold waistcoat*

round needle, then slip, one at a time, each of these 5 sts.
over the yarn round needle loop, p.2, B.Cr., p.3.
17th row: P.7, B.Cr., p.4.
19th row: P.6, B.Cr., p.5.
21st row: P.5, B.Cr., p.6.
23rd row: P.4, B.Cr., p.7.
25th row: P.3, B.Cr., p.2, make 5 sts. out of next st., as 13th
row, p.5.
26th row: K.5, p.5, k.3, p.2, k.3.
27th row: P.3, F.Cr., p.2, work 5 sts. tog. as 15th row, p.5.
28th row: As 2nd row.
These 28 rows form the pattern.

Back

With 3 mm (No. 11: 2) needles, cast on 130
[138:146:154:162:170] sts.
Work 5 cm (2 in) k.1, p.1 rib, inc. 8 sts. evenly across last
row. 138 [146:154:162:170:178] sts.
Change to 3¼ mm (No. 10: 3) needles, and continue in pattern
placing panels thus:
1st row: (right side) **Panel A over 20 [24:28:32:36:40] sts.,
Panel B over next 8 sts., p.2, Panel C over next 24 sts., Panel
B over next 8 sts.**, Panel D over centre 14 sts., *** Tw.2
K., Panel B over next 4 sts., p.2, Panel C over next 24 sts.,
Panel B over next 8 sts., p.2, Panel A over 20
[24:28:32:36:40] sts. ***
Continue in pattern with panels as now set until work
measures 35 cm (14 in) ending after a wrong side row.

Shape Armholes

Cast off 8 sts. at beginning of next 2 rows; 4 sts. at beginning
of following 4 rows. 106 [114:122:130:138:146] sts.
Continue in pattern without shaping until armholes measure
18 [19:20:20:23:23] cm (7 [7½:8:8:9:9] in) ending after a wrong
side row.

Shape Shoulders

Cast off 7 [8:9:10:11:12] sts. at beginning of next 6 rows; 8
sts. at beginning of next 2 rows. Leave remaining 48
[50:52:54:56:58] sts. on spare needle.

Left Front

With 3 mm (No. 11: 2) needles, cast on 60 [64:68:72:76:80]
sts.
Work 5 cm (2 in) in k.1, p.1 rib, inc. 4 sts. evenly across last
row. 64 [68:72:76:80:84] sts.
Change to 3¼ mm (No. 10: 3) needles and continue in pattern,
placing panels thus:
1st row: Work from ** to ** on back pattern p.2.
Continue in this way, having last 2 sts. on right side rows as
p.2, and first 2 sts. on wrong side rows as k.2, until front
matches back to armhole ending after the same pattern row.

Shape Armhole

Cast off 8 sts. at beginning of next row; 4 sts. at beginning of following 2 alternate rows.

Continue straight until armhole measures 5 cm (2 in) ending after a right side row.

Shape Neck

Cast off 10 sts. at beginning of next row, then cast off 2 sts. at beginning of following wrong side rows, 4 times. Dec. 1 st. at neck edge on every row until 29 [32:35:38:41:44] sts. remain.

Continue straight until armhole matches back to shoulder, ending at side edge.

Shape Shoulder

Cast off 7 [8:9:10:11:12] sts. at beginning of next row and following 2 alternate rows; 8 sts. at beginning of following alternate row.

Right Front

As left front, reversing shapings and working panels from *** to *** on back pattern, having the p.2 at beginning of right side rows and k.2 at end of wrong side rows.

Front Bands

With 3 mm (No. 11: 2) needles, cast on 11 sts.
1st row: K.2, *p.1, k.1; rep. from * to last st., k.1.
2nd row: K.1, *p.1, k.1; rep. from * to end.

Repeat last 2 rows until band, slightly stretched, fits left front from cast on edge to beginning of neck shaping. Leave sts. on spare needle.

Mark this band with pins to represent buttons, the lowest to be 4 rows from cast on edge, the top one to be level with centre of neckband and the remaining 6 pins to be spaced equally between.

Now work the right front band to match left, working buttonholes to correspond with the pinned positions thus:
1st row: Rib 4, cast off 3, rib to end.
2nd row: Rib 4, cast on 3, rib to end.

When buttonhole band matches button band, leave sts. on spare needle.

Armbands

Join shoulder seams.

With right side of work facing, using 3 mm (No. 11: 2) needles, pick up and k. 132 [136:140:140:144:144] sts. evenly round armhole edge.

Work 10 rows k.1, p.1 rib, dec. 1 st. at both ends of every right side row. Cast off sts. loosely in rib.

Neckband

Sew on front bands.

With right side of work facing, using 3 mm (No. 11: 2) needles, rib 11 sts. of front band, pick up and k. 56 [60:62:62:68:68] sts. to right shoulder, k. 48 [50:52:54:56:58] sts. from back neck, pick up and k. 57 [61:63:63:69:69] sts. from left front neck, rib 11 sts. of front band. 183 [193:199:201:215:217] sts.

Work 9 rows in k.1, p.1 rib working buttonhole on 4th and 5th rows to correspond with previous buttonholes.
Cast off sts. loosely in rib.

To Make Up

Join side seams. Press seams lightly, following pressing instructions on ball disc.
Sew on buttons.

PATTERN 17: LADY'S TABARD

The intricacy of the patterning on this useful tunic is concentrated at the centre front and back, making it a moderately easy piece for a beginner to Aran knitting.

Materials

600 [650:700:750] g Lister/Lee Aran quality yarn
A pair each $3\frac{3}{4}$ mm and $4\frac{1}{2}$ mm (No. 9 and No. 7 UK: 4 and 6 USA) knitting needles
A cable needle
A 4·5 mm crochet hook

Measurements

To fit 81 [86:91:97] cm (32 [34:36:38] in) bust; length, 66 [67:68:69] cm (26 [$26\frac{1}{2}$:$26\frac{3}{4}$:27] in)

Tension

19 sts. to 10 cm (4 in) over stocking stitch

Special Abbreviations

Tw.2., twist 2 sts. thus: k. second st. on left hand needle, then k. first st. and slip both loops off together.
M.B., make bobble thus: k. into front, back, front, back, front of next st., (making 5 sts. out of 1), k. next st., turn and p.5, turn and k.5, turn and p.5, next slip 2nd, 3rd, 4th and 5th sts. over the 1st st. and k. into back of the bobble st.— bobble made.
Note: 2 sts. are required to make this type of bobble.
Sl. 1 f., slip next st. to front on cable needle.
Sl. 1 b., slip next st. to back on cable needle.

Panel A   Gull Stitch 9 sts.

1st row: (right side) K.
2nd row: P.
3rd row: Slip 3 sts. to back on cable needle, k.1, then k.3 from cable needle, k.1, slip next st. to front on cable needle, k.3, then k.1 from cable needle.
4th row: P.
These 4 rows form the pattern.

Panel B   Irish Moss Diamonds with 3 Rib Sts. and Bobbles 33 sts.

1st row: (right side) K.6, p.1, k.4, (k.1, p.1) 5 times, k.1 t.b.l., k.4, p.1, k.6.
2nd row: P.6, k.1, p.4, (p.1, k.1) 5 times, p.1 t.b.l., p.4, k.1, p.6.

110 *Lady's tabard, pattern 17*

3rd row: K.6, p.1, k.3, (sl. 1 b., k.1 t.b.l., p. the sl.st) 3 times, k.1, (sl. 1 f., p.1, k. the sl.st. t.b.l.) 3 times, k.3, p.1, k.6.
4th row: P.6, k.1, p.3, (p.1 t.b.l., k.1) 3 times, p.1, k.1, (p.1 t.b.l., k.1) twice, p.1 t.b.l., p.3, k.1, p.6.
5th row: K.2, M.B., k.2, p.1, k.2, (sl. 1 b., k.1 t.b.l., p. the sl.st.) 3 times, k.1, p.1, k.1, (sl. 1 f., p.1, k. the sl.st. t.b.l.) 3 times, k.2, p.1, k.2, M.B., k.2.
6th row: P.6, k.1, p.2, (p.1 t.b.l., k.1) 3 times, (p.1, k.1) twice, p.1, (p.1 t.b.l., k.1) twice, p.2, k.1, p.6.
7th row: K.6, p.1, k.1, (sl.1 b., k.1 t.b.l., p. the sl.st.) 3 times, (k.1, p.1) twice, k.1, (sl.1 f., p.1, k. the sl.st t.b.l.) 3 times, k.1, p.1, k.6.
8th row: P.6, k.1, p.1, (p.1 t.b.l., k.1) 3 times, (p.1, k.1) 3 times, (p.1 t.b.l., k.1) twice, p.1 t.b.l., p.1, k.1, p.6.
9th row: K.6, p.1, (sl.1 b., k.1 t.b.l., p. the sl.st) 3 times, (k.1, p.1) 3 times, k.1, (sl.1 f., p.1, k. the sl.st. t.b.l.) 3 times, p.1, k.6.
10th row: P.6, k.1, (p.1 t.b.l., k.1) 3 times, (p.1, k.1) 4 times, (p.1 t.b.l., k.1) twice, p.1 t.b.l., k.1, p.6.
11th row: K.6, p.1 sl.1 f., k.1, k. the sl.st. t.b.l., (sl.1 f., p.1, k. the sl.st. t.b.l.) twice, (p.1, k.1) 3 times, p.1, (sl.1 b., k.1 t.b.l., p. the sl.st) twice, sl.1 b., k.1 t.b.l., k. the sl.st., p.1, k.6.
12th row: P.6, k.1, p.1, (p.1 t.b.l., k.1) 3 times, (p.1, k.1) 3 times, (p.1 t.b.l., k.1) twice, p.1 t.b.l., p.1, k.1, p.6.
13th row: K.2, M.B., k.2, p.1, k.1, sl.1 f., k.1, k. the sl.st. t.b.l., (sl.1 f., p.1, k. the sl.st. t.b.l.) twice, (p.1, k.1) twice, p.1, (sl.1 b., k.1 t.b.l., p. the sl.st.) twice, sl.1 b., k.1 t.b.l., k. the sl.st., k.1, p.1, k.2, M.B., k.2.
14th row: P.6, k.1, p.2, (p.1 t.b.l., k.1) 3 times, (p.1, k.1) twice, (p.1 t.b.l., k.1) twice, p.1 t.b.l., p.2, k.1, p.6.
15th row: K.6, p.1, k.2, sl.1 f., k.1, k. the sl.st. t.b.l., (sl.1 f., p.1, k. the sl.st. t.b.l.) twice, p.1, k.1, p.1, (sl.1 b., k.1 t.b.l., p. the sl.st.) twice, sl.1 b., k.1 t.b.l., k. the sl.st., k.2, p.1, k.6.
16th row: P.6, k.1, p.3, (p.1 t.b.l., k.1) 3 times, p.1, k.1, (p.1 t.b.l., k.1) twice, p.1 t.b.l., p.3, k.1, p.6.
17th row: K.6, p.1, k.3, sl.1 f., k.1, k. the sl.st. t.b.l., (sl.1 f., p.1, k. the sl.st. t.b.l.) twice, p.1, (sl.1 b., k.1 t.b.l., p. the sl.st.) twice, sl.1 b., k.1 t.b.l., k. the sl.st., k.3, p.1, k.6.
18th row: As 2nd row.
These 18 rows form the pattern.

Back Centre Panel
With 4½ mm (No. 7: 6) needles, cast on 93 [97:101:105] sts.
Work in pattern, placing panels thus:
1st row: (K.1, p.1) twice, p. 5 [7:9:11] sts., *p.2, Tw.2, p.2, Panel A over next 9 sts., p.2, Tw.2, p.2*, Panel B over centre 33 sts., rep. from * to *, p. 5 [7:9:11] sts., (p.1, k.1) twice.
2nd row: (P.1, k.1) twice, k. 5 [7:9:11] sts., *k.2, p.2, k.2, Panel A over 9 sts., k.2, p.2, k.2*, Panel B over centre 33 sts., rep. from * to *, k. 5 [7:9:11] sts., (k.1, p.1) twice.
Continue in pattern with panels as now set until work measures 18 cm (7 in) ending after a wrong side row.

Shape Sides

Next row: (K.1, p.1) twice, p. 3 [5:7:9] sts., slip 1, k.1, p.s.s.o., pattern to last 9 [11:13:15] sts., k. 2 tog., p. 3 [5:7:9], (p.1, k.1) twice. 91 [95:99:103] sts.

Continue in pattern for a further 5 cm (2 in) ending after a wrong side row.

Next row: (K.1, p.1) twice, p. 2 [4:6:8] sts., slip 1, k.1, p.s.s.o., pattern to last 8 [10:12:14] sts., k. 2 tog., p. 2[4:6:8] sts., (p.1, k.1) twice.

Continue in pattern for a further 5 cm (2 in) ending after a wrong side row.

Next row: (K.1, p.1) twice, p. 1 [3:5:7] sts., slip 1, k.1, p.s.s.o., pattern to last 7 [9:11:13] sts., k. 2 tog., p. 1 [3:5:7] sts., (p.1, k.1) twice. 87 [91:95:99] sts.

Continue straight in pattern until work measures 47 cm (18½ in) ending after a wrong side row.

Shape Armholes

Cast off 4 [5:6:7] sts. at beginning of next 2 rows. Dec. 1 st. at both ends of next row and following alternate rows until 75 [77:79:81] sts. remain. **

Continue straight until armholes measure 19 [20:21:22] cm (7½ [8:8¼:8¾] in) ending after a wrong side row.

Shape Shoulders

Cast off 5 sts. at beginning of next 6 rows; 5 [6:7:8] sts. at beginning of following 2 rows. Leave remaining 35 sts. on spare needle.

Front

Work as back to **.

Continue straight until armholes measure 12 [13:14:15] cm (4¾ [5:5½:6] in) ending after a wrong side row.

Shape Neck

Next row: Pattern 28 [29:30:31] sts., turn and complete this side first.

Dec. 1 st. at neck edge on next 4 rows, then dec. 1 st. at neck edge on following 4 alternate rows. 20 [21:22:23] sts.

Continue straight until armhole matches back to shoulder, ending after a wrong side row.

Shape Shoulder

Cast off 5 sts. at beginning of next row and following 2 alternate rows; 5 [6:7:8] sts. at beginning of following alternate row. With right side of work facing, slip centre 19 sts. on to spare needle. Join yarn and pattern to end of row. Complete this side to match first side, reversing shapings.

Side Panels (Make 2)

With 4½ mm (No. 7: 6) needles, cast on 21 sts.

Work in reverse stocking stitch (p. side is right side) until panel measures 47 cm (18½ in), matching side edge to beginning of armhole shaping.

Cast off sts.

Neckband

Join right shoulder seam.

With right side of work facing, using 3¾ mm (No. 9: 4) needles, pick up and k. 23 sts. down left front neck edge, k. 19 sts. from front neck, pick up and k. 23 sts. to right shoulder, k. 35 sts. from back neck. 100 sts.

Work 6 rows k.1, p.1 rib. Cast off sts. loosely in rib.

To Make Up

With right side of work facing, beginning at armhole, work 1 row double crochet along right front edge of centre panel to cast on edge, *do not turn*, work 1 row shrimp stitch (d.c. worked from left to right) along this d.c. row. Fasten off. Work 1 row d.c. and 1 row shrimp stitch along left front edge and right and left side edges of back centre panel.

Join left shoulder and neckband seams.

Sew the side panels to front edge, concealing seam behind the shrimp stitch edging.

Armbands

With right side of work facing, using 3¾ mm (No. 9: 4) needles, pick up and k. 120 [124:128:132] sts. evenly round armhole edge, including side panel. Work 6 rows k.1, p.1 rib. Cast off sts. in rib.

Join other edge of side panels to back, concealing seam behind the shrimp stitch edging.

Press stocking stitch and seams, omitting ribbed sections.

III *Detail of tabard centre panel, pattern 17*

PATTERN 18: LADY'S HAT

The simple line of cable with bobble pattern stands out against the smooth background of reverse stocking stitch on this warm pull-on hat.

Materials

150g Emu Aran yarn

Note: If working hat with scarf and mitts, patterns 19 and 20, a total of 450g is required

A pair each 3¼ mm and 4½ mm (No. 10 and No. 7 UK: 3 and 6 USA) knitting needles

A cable needle

4.5 mm crochet hook (optional)

Measurement

To fit 55 cm (21¾ in) head size

Tension

19 sts. to 10 cm (4 in) over stocking stitch

Special Abbreviations

B.Cr., back cross thus: slip next st. to back on cable needle, k.2, then p.1 from cable needle.

F.Cr., front cross thus: slip next 2 sts. to front on cable needle, p.1, then k.2 from cable needle.

M.B., make bobble thus: (K.1, y.fwd.) twice, k.1, all in next st., (making 5 sts. out of 1 st.), turn and p.5, turn and k.5, turn and p. 2 tog., p.1, p. 2 tog., turn and slip 1, k. 2 tog., p.s.s.o.—bobble made.

To Make

With 3¼ mm (No. 10: 3) needles, cast on 110 sts.

Work 8 cm (3¼ in) k.1, p.1 rib, inc. 1 st. at both ends of last row. 112 sts.

Change to 4½ mm (No. 7: 6) needles and continue in pattern, placing panels thus:

1st row: (wrong side) K.1, *k.3, p.2, k.1, p.2, k.3; rep. from * to last st., k.1.

2nd row: K.1, *p.3, slip next 3 sts. to back on cable needle, k.2, then slip the p. st. back on to left hand needle and p. this st., then k.2 from cable needle, p.3; rep. from * to last st., k.1.

3rd row: As 1st row.

4th row: K.1, *p.2, B.Cr., p.1, F.Cr., p.2; rep. from * to last st., k.1.

5th row: K.1, *k.2, p.2, k.3, p.2, k.2; rep. from * to last st., k.1.

6th row: K.1, *p.1, B.Cr., p.3, F.Cr., p.1; rep. from * to last st., k.1.

7th row: K.1, *k.1, p.2, k.5, p.2, k.1; rep. from * to last st., k.1.

8th row: K.1, *p.1, k.2, p.2, M.B., p.2, k.2, p.1; rep. from * to last st., k.1.

9th row: As 7th row.

10th row: K.1, *p.1, F.Cr., p.3, B.Cr., p.1; rep. from * to last st., k.1.

11th row: As 5th row.

12th row: K.1, *p.2, F.Cr., p.1, B.Cr., p.2; rep. from * to last st., k.1.

Repeat these 12 rows until work measures 16 cm (6¼ in) from last rib row, ending after nearest 3rd pattern row.

Shape Top

Next row: K.1, *p. 2 tog., B.Cr., p.1, F.Cr., p. 2 tog.; rep. from * to last st., k.1.

Next row: K.1, *k.1, p.2, k.3, p.2, k.1; rep. from * to last st., k.1.

Next row: K.1, *p. 2 tog., k.1, p.3, k.1, p. 2 tog.; rep. from * to last st., k.1.

Next row: K.1, *k.1, p.1, k.3, p.1, k.1; rep. from * to last st., k.1.

Next row: K.1, *p.1, k.1, p.3, k.1, p.1; rep. from * to last st., k.1.

Repeat last 2 rows until work measures 26 cm (10¼ in).

Break yarn with a long end. Thread end through remaining sts., draw up and tighten securely.

To Make Up

Using long end, join back seam, reversing seam at lower edge

112 *Lady's hat, mitts and scarf set,*
patterns 18, 19 and 20

of rib for brim.

Use crochet hook to work a chain of approximately 10 cm (4 in). Fasten off. A cord may also be made, if preferred, by casting on 23 sts. with 3¼ mm (No. 10: 3) needles, then cast off the sts. Cut remaining yarn into 20 cm (8 in) lengths and form into a tassel.

Press hat omitting ribbed section. Attach cord to tassel and sew other end of cord to centre of hat crown. Fold half ribbed section to right side to form the brim.

PATTERN 19: LADY'S MITTS

Warm and fashionable, these mitts match the pull-on hat in the previous pattern, page 131.

Materials

100g Emu Aran yarn
A pair each 3¼ mm and 4½ mm (No. 10 and No. 7 UK: 3 and 6 USA) knitting needles
A cable needle

Measurement

To fit 18 cm (7 in) wrist to finger tip (adjustable)

Tension
19 sts. to 10 cm over stocking stitch

Special Abbreviations
B.Cr., back cross thus: slip next st. to back on cable needle, k.2, then p.1 from cable needle.

F.Cr., front cross thus: slip next 2 sts. to front on cable needle, p.1, then k.2 from cable needle.

M.B., make bobble thus: (K.1, y.fwd.) twice, k.1, all in next st., (making 5 sts. out of 1 st.), turn and p.5, turn and k.5, turn and p. 2 tog., p.1, p. 2 tog., turn and slip 1, k. 2 tog., p.s.s.o.—bobble made.

To Make
With 3¼ mm (No. 10: 3) needles, cast on 38 sts.

Work 16 rows k.1, p.1 rib.

Change to 4½ mm (No. 7: 6) needles and pattern thus:

1st row: (wrong side) K.4, *k.3, p.2, k.1, p.2, k.3*, k.8, rep. from * to *, k.4.

2nd row: K.1, p.3, *p.3, slip next 3 sts. to back on cable needle, k.2, then slip the p. st. back on to left hand needle and p. it, then k.2 from cable needle, p.3*, p.8, rep. from * to *, p.3, k.1.

Inc. for Thumb
3rd row: K.4, rep. from * to * on 1st row, k.2, inc. in next st., k.1, inc. in next st., k.3, rep. from * to * on 1st row, k.4.

4th row: K.1, p.3, *p.2, B.Cr., p.1, F.Cr., p.2*, p.10, rep. from * to *, p.3, k.1.

5th row: K.4, *k.2, p.2, k.3, p.2, k.2*, k.10, rep. from * to *, k.4.

6th row: K.1, p.3, *p.1, B.Cr., p.3, F.Cr., p.1*, p.10, rep. from * to *, p.3, k.1.

7th row: K.4, *k.1, p.2, k.5, p.2, k.1*, k.2, inc. in next st., k.3, inc. in next st., k.3, rep. from * to *, k.4.

8th row: K.1, p.3, *p.1, k.2, p.2, M.B., p.2, k.2, p.1*, p.12, rep. from * to *, p.3, k.1.

9th row: K.4, rep. from * to * on 7th row, k.12, rep. from * to * on 7th row, k.4.

10th row: K.1, p.3, *p.1, F.Cr., p.3, B.Cr., p.1*, p.12, rep. from * to *, p.3, k.1.

11th row: K.4, rep. from * to * on 5th row, k.2, inc. in next st., k.5, inc. in next st., k.3, rep. from * to * on 5th row, k.4.

12th row: K.1, p.3, *p.2, F.Cr., p.1, B.Cr., p.2*, p.14, rep. from * to *, p.3, k.1.

Repeating the 12 pattern rows between * to *, continue in pattern and inc. every 4th row as before to 48 sts. Work 1 row.

Thumb
Next row: Work 30 sts., cast on 1 st., turn.

K.1, p.12, cast on 1 st., turn.

Work 11 rows more on these 14 sts.

Next row: *K. 2 tog.; rep. from * to end.

P. 1 row. Break yarn and thread end through remaining sts. and draw up to secure.

With 18 sts. on right hand needle, pick up and k. 1 st. from both sides of base of thumb and work remaining 18 sts. Continue in pattern on these 38 sts. until 40 pattern rows in all have been worked. Length may be adjusted here if required.

Shape Top

Keeping pattern correct where possible between shapings, dec. in next row and every following alternate row thus:

1st row: *K.1, slip 1, k.1, p.s.s.o., pattern 13 sts., k. 2 tog., k.1; rep. from * to end.

3rd row: *K.1, slip 1, k.1, p.s.s.o., pattern 11 sts., k. 2 tog., k.1; rep. from * to end.

Continue in this way until 18 sts. remain.

Cast off sts.

Work second mitt in the same way.

To Make Up

Join thumb seam. Join side and top seams.

Press work lightly omitting ribbed cuffs.

PATTERN 20: LADY'S SCARF

The cable and bobble pattern of the hat and mitts borders a panel of Trinity pattern stitch to make a matching scarf which is suitable for all members of the family.

Materials

250g Emu Aran yarn
A pair of 4½ mm (No. 7 UK: 6 USA) knitting needles
A cable needle

Measurements

Length, 122 cm (48 in) not including fringe
Width, 24 cm (9¼ in)

Special Abbreviations

B.Cr., back cross thus: slip next st. to back on cable needle, k.2, then p.1 from cable needle.

F.Cr., front cross thus: slip next 2 sts. to front on cable needle, p.1, then k.2 from cable needle.

M.B. make bobble thus: (k.1, y.fwd.) twice, k.1, all in next st. (making 5 sts. out of 1 st.), turn and p.5, turn and k.5, turn and p. 2 tog., p.1, p. 2 tog., turn and slip 1, k. 2 tog., p.s.s.o.,—bobble made.

Panel A Trinity Pattern 4 sts.

1st row: (wrong side) P. 3 tog., k.1, p.1, k.1 all in next st.
2nd row: P.
3rd row: K.1, p.1, k.1 all in next st., p. 3 tog.
4th row: P.

These 4 rows form the pattern.

113 *Detail of panel on scarf, pattern 20*

To Make

With 4½ mm (No. 7: 6) needles, cast on 50 sts.

Work in pattern, placing panels thus:

1st row: (wrong side) K.2, *k.3, p.2, k.1, p.2, k.3*, p.2, Panel A over next 20 sts., p.2, rep. from * to *, k.2.

2nd row: K.2, *p.3, slip next 3 sts. to back on cable needle, k.2, slip the p. st. back on to left hand needle and p. this st., then k.2 from cable needle, p.3*, k.2, Panel A over next 20 sts., k.2, rep. from * to *, k.2.

3rd row: As 1st row.

4th row: K.2, *p.2, B.Cr., p.1, F.Cr., p.2*, k.2, Panel A over next 20 sts., k.2, rep. from * to *, k.2.

5th row: K.2, *k.2, p.2, k.3, p.2, k.2*, p.2, Panel A over next 20 sts., p.2, rep. from * to *, k.2.

6th row: K.2, *p.1, B.Cr., p.3, F.Cr., p.1*, k.2, Panel A over next 20 sts., k.2, rep. from * to *, k.2.

7th row: K.2, *k.1, p.2, k.5, p.2, k.1*, p.2, Panel A over next 20 sts., p.2, rep. from * to *, k.2.

8th row: K.2, *p.1, k.2, p.2, M.B., p.2, k.2, p.1*, k.2, Panel A over next 20 sts., k.2, rep. from * to *, k.2.

9th row: K.2, rep. from * to * on 7th row, p.2, Panel A over next 20 sts., p.2, rep. from * to * on 7th row, k.2.

10th row: K.2, *p.1, F.Cr., p.3, B.Cr., p.1*, k.2, Panel A over next 20 sts., k.2, rep. from * to *, k.2.

11th row: K.2, rep. from * to * on 5th row, p.2, Panel A over next 20 sts., p.2, rep. from * to * on 5th pattern row, k.2.

12th row: K.2, *p.2, F.Cr., p.1, B.Cr., p.2*, k.2, Panel A over next 20 sts., k.2, rep. from * to *, k.2.

Repeat these 12 rows until scarf measures 122 cm (48 in) or required length. Cast off sts.

Cut remaining yarn into 20 cm (8 in) lengths and fringe narrow ends. Press work lightly.

PATTERN 21: SQUARE CUSHION COVER

A simple shape, worked from small squares of medallion cables on reverse stocking stitch background. Many other cable patterns would be suitable for this type of cushion cover and an interesting pattern may be obtained by working a different cable pattern for each square.

Materials

300g Emu Aran yarn

A pair 4½ mm (No. 7 UK: 6 USA) knitting needles

A cable needle

4·5 mm crochet hook

A 35 cm (14 in) zip fastener

1 button approximately 2·5 cm (1 in) diameter

Measurements

To fit 35 cm (14 in) cushion pad

Tension

19 sts. to 10 cm (4 in) over stocking stitch

114 *A collection of cushions, patterns 21, 22 and 23*

Special Abbreviations

C. 4 F., cable 4 front thus: slip next 2 sts. to front on cable needle, k.2, then k.2 from cable needle.

C. 4 B., cable 4 back thus: slip next 2 sts. to back on cable needle, k.2, then k.2 from cable needle.

To Make

With 4½ mm (No. 7: 6) needles, cast on 42 sts.

Work in pattern, placing sts. thus:

1st row: k.1, *p.4, k.8; rep. from * twice more, p.4, k.1.

2nd and foll. alt. rows: K.1, *k.4, p.8; rep. from * twice more, k.5.

3rd row: K.1, *p.4, C. 4 B., C. 4 F.; rep. from * to last 5 sts., p.4, k.1.

5th row: As 1st row.

7th row: K.1, *p.4, C. 4 F., C. 4 B.; rep. from * to last 5 sts., p.4, k.1.

8th row: As 2nd row.

These 8 rows form the pattern.

Continue in pattern until piece measures 18 cm (7 in). Cast off.

Work 7 more squares in the same way.

To Make Up

Join cast off edge of one square to side edge of second square.

115 *The square cushion, pattern 21*

Join the second square cast off edge to the side of the third square, then join to fourth square in sequence, joining last seam to form one large square. Join remaining four pieces together to form a second large square.

With right side of one large square facing, work 1 row double crochet round outer edge, working 3 d.c. at each corner. *Do not turn*, work 1 row shrimp stitch (d.c. worked from left to right) round this d.c. row. Fasten off.

Sew three sides of back of cushion to front, concealing seam behind shrimp stitch edging.

With 4½ mm (No. 7: 6) needles, cast on 9 sts. Work in reverse st.-st (p. side is right side) until piece is large enough to cover the button. Cast off sts. leaving long end. Using the end, thread through all round the button cover, enclosing the button. Draw up tightly and secure.

Press work lightly. Sew the covered button to centre of front. Sew zip fastener to open edge. Insert cushion pad and close fastener.

PATTERN 22: OBLONG CUSHION COVER

Heavily embossed branch cable forms the centre panel of this rectangular shaped cushion cover.

Materials
300g Emu Aran yarn
A pair 4½ mm (No. 7 UK: 6 USA) knitting needles
A cable needle
A 35 cm (14 in) zip fastener

Measurements
To fit a cushion pad, 35 cm (14 in) deep and 40 cm (16 in) wide

Tension
19 sts. to 10 cm (4 in) wide over stocking stitch

Special Abbreviations
Cr. 6 L., cross 6 sts. left thus: slip next 2 sts. to front on cable needle, k.2, p.2, then k.2 from cable needle.
Cr. 6 R., cross 6 sts. right thus: slip next 4 sts. to back on cable needle, k.2, then p.2, k.2 from cable needle.

Panel A   Branch Cable Pattern 18 sts.
1st row: K.1, p.2, k.2, p.2, k.4, p.2, k.2, p.2, k.1.
2nd row: P.1, k.2, p.2, k.2, p.4, k.2, p.2, k.2, p.1.
3rd to 6th rows: Rep. 1st and 2nd rows twice.
7th row: K.1, p.2, Cr. 6 R., Cr. 6 L., p.2, k.1.
8th row: As 2nd row.
9th to 11th rows: Rep. 1st and 2nd rows, then 1st row once more.
12th and 14th rows: P.1, k.16, p.1.
13th and 15th rows: K.
16th row: As 12th row.
These 16 rows form the pattern.

Panel B   Small Cable Pattern 10 sts.
1st row: (right side) (P.2, k.2) twice, p.2.
2nd row: (K.2, p.2) twice, k.2.
3rd row: P.2, slip next 4 sts. to front on cable needle, k.2, slip
the p.2 sts. back on to left hand needle and p.2 these sts.,
then k.2 from cable needle, p.2.
4th row: As 2nd row.
5th to 8th rows: Rep. 1st and 2nd rows twice.
These 8 rows form the pattern.

Panel C   Trinity Pattern 4 sts.
1st row: (right side) P.
2nd row: P. 3 tog., k.1, p.1, k.1 all in next st.
3rd row: P.
4th row: K.1, p.1, k.1, all in next st., p. 3 tog.
These 4 rows form the pattern.

Panel D   Spiral Rib 7 sts.
1st row: (right side) P.2, k. 2 tog., do not slip loops off left
hand needle but k. in first of these 2 loops then slip them off
left hand needle together, k.1, p.2.
2nd row: K.2, p.3, k.2.
3rd row: P.2, k.1, k. in back of second st. on left hand needle,
then k. first and second sts. together t.b.l. and slip both loops
off together, p.2.
4th row: As 2nd row.
These 4 rows form the pattern.

To Make
With 4½ mm (No. 7: 6) needles, cast on 92 sts.   **116** *The oblong cushion, pattern 22*

Work in pattern, placing sts. thus:

1st row: (right side) P.6, Panel D over 7 sts., k.1, Panel C over 12 sts., k.1, Panel B over 10 sts., Panel A over centre 18 sts., Panel B over 10 sts., k.1, Panel C over 12 sts., k.1, Panel D over 7 sts., p.6.

2nd row: K.6, Panel D over 7 sts., p.1, Panel C over 12 sts., p.1, Panel B over 10 sts., Panel A over 18 sts., Panel B over 10 sts., p.1, Panel C over 12 sts., p.1, Panel D over 7 sts., k.6.

Continue in pattern with panels as now set until work measures 71 cm (28 in) ending after a wrong side row. Cast off sts.

To Make Up

Fold cushion piece in half across width. Join one narrow end. Press work lightly.

Cut remaining yarn into 16 cm (6¼ in) lengths. With right side of work facing, using two strands together, work fringe along three doubled edges, then along front edge of open end. Sew zip fastener in open end. Insert cushion pad and close fastener.

PATTERN 23: BOLSTER-SHAPED CUSHION COVER

This cover has a beautiful textured pattern of woven basket stitch.

Materials

350g Emu Aran yarn
A pair each 4 mm and 4½ mm (No. 8 and No. 7 UK: 5 and 6 USA) knitting needles
A cable needle
A 50 cm (20 in) zip fastener

Measurements

Width, 51 cm (20 in); diameter, 23 cm (9 in)

Tension

19 sts. to 10 cm (4 in) over stocking stitch

Special Abbreviations

B.Cr., back cross thus: slip next st. to back on cable needle, k.2, then p.1 from cable needle.
F.Cr., front cross thus: slip next 2 sts. to front on cable needle, p.1, then k.2 from cable needle.

To Make

With 4½ mm (No. 7: 6) needles, cast on 110 sts.
Continue in pattern thus:
1st row: (wrong side) K.2, *p.4, k.2; rep. from * to end.
2nd row: P.2, *slip next 2 sts. to back on cable needle, k.2, then k.2 from cable needle, p.2; rep. from * to end.
3rd row and foll. alt. rows: K. the k. sts. and p. the p. sts. as they present themselves.

4th row: P.1, *B.Cr., F.Cr.; rep. from * to end, p.1.
6th row: P.1, k.2, p.2, *slip next 2 sts. to front on cable needle, k.2, then k.2 from cable needle, p.2; rep. from * ending last repeat, k.2, p.1.
8th row: P.1, *F.Cr., B.Cr.; rep. from * ending last repeat, p.1.
These 8 rows form the pattern.
Continue in pattern until piece measures 61 cm (24 in) ending after a wrong side row.

End Panels (Make 2)

With 4 mm (No. 8: 5) needles, cast on 24 sts.
** *1st row and foll. alt. rows:* K.
2nd row: P. to last 2 sts., turn.
4th row: P. to last 4 sts., turn.
6th row: P. to last 6 sts., turn.
8th row: P. to last 8 sts., turn.
Continue in this manner, leaving 2 more sts. before turning on following alternate rows until the row 'P. to last 20 sts., turn' has been worked.
Next row: (right side) K.4.
Next row: K. to end. **
Repeat from ** to ** until 8 panels in all have been worked.
Cast off.

To Make Up

Join the end panels into a disc shape by seaming the cast on and cast off edges. Sew the panels to the side edges of the main piece. Make two tassels from the remaining yarn and sew one to centre of each end panel.
Sew zip fastener in opening. Insert cushion pad. Close zip fastener.

117 *Detail of the bolster cushion, pattern 23*

CONVERSION CHART FOR KNITTING NEEDLES AND CROCHET HOOKS

Knitting Needles

U.K. Old sizes	Metric	U.S.A.	Continental
000	10 mm	15	9 mm
00	9 mm	13	8½ mm
0	8 mm	12	8 mm
1	7½ mm	11	7½
2	7 mm	10½	7 mm
3	6½ mm	10	6½
4	6 mm	9	6 mm
5	5½ mm	8	5½ mm
6	5 mm	7	5 mm
7	4½ mm	6	4½ mm
8	4 mm	5	4 mm
9	3¾ mm	4	3½ mm
10	3¼ mm	3	–
11	3 mm	2	3 mm
12	2¾ mm	1	2½ mm
13	2¼ mm	0	–
14	2 mm	00	2 mm

Crochet Hooks

U.K.	U.S.A.	Continental
7 mm	K/10½	7 mm
6·5 mm	J/10	6·5 mm
6 mm	I/9	6 mm
5·5 mm	H/8	5·5 mm
5 mm	–	5 mm
4·5 mm	G/6	4·5 mm
4 mm	F/5	4 mm
3·5 mm	E/4	3·5 mm
3 mm	C/2	3 mm
2·5 mm	B/1	2·5 mm

BIBLIOGRAPHY

The Batsford Book of Knitting and Crochet, Ann Stearns, Batsford, 1981.

Butler, Winifred, *Knitting*, Teach Yourself Books, Hodder and Stoughton, 1979.

Dixon, Margaret, *The Wool Book*, Hamlyn, 1979.

*Thomas, Mary, *Book of Knitting Patterns*, Hodder and Stoughton, 1935.

Thompson, Gladys, *Patterns for Guernseys, Jerseys and Arans*, Dover Publications, 1975.

Walker, Barbara, *A Treasury of Knitting Patterns*, Charles Scribner's Sons, New York, 1968.

*This book is available as a Dover reprint (0-486-22818-5).

INDEX